DISCOVERING
GOD

THE SPIRITUAL JOURNEY OF LIFE

by

MAULANA WAHIDUDDIN KHAN

Translated by:
Prof. Farida Khanum

Edited by:
Dr. Naghma Siddiqi & Maria Khan

Acknowledgment

This edition is published with permission from CPS International (Center for Peace and Spirituality), New Delhi, which granted the Ghamidi Center of Islamic Learning (GCIL) the non-exclusive right to publish and distribute works of Maulana Wahiduddin Khan.

First Published By:
CPS International (Center for Peace and Spirituality)
New Delhi, India

Publisher (This Edition)

ISBN: 978-1-966600-39-8

Address: 3620 N Josey Ln, Suite 230 Carrollton, TX 75007
Website: www.ghamidicenter.com
Email: info@ghamidicenter.com

CONTRIBUTORS TO THE GCIL EDITION
Project Director | Farhan Saiyed
Layout Supervision | Muhammad Irtaza Ajmal
Typesetting & Layout Design | Tallal Bin Nasir

TABLE OF CONTENTS

CHAPTER 02

PURIFICATION OF THE SELF 61

CHAPTER 04

REMEMBRANCE OF GOD 144

FOREWORD

The theme of this book is the realization of God. Several chapters have been devoted to this subject. The realization of God is the essence of religion. Realization of God (ma'rifah) is the beginning as well as the end of religion. The position of ma'rifah in God's religion is that of the seed. Just as a seed grows gradually into a full tree, similarly ma'rifah shapes the entire personality of a person. Without ma'rifah, religion is reduced to a spiritless form. With ma'rifah, religion is like a lush green tree and without it, religion becomes like a dried up tree. If religion is the body, ma'rifah is its spirit.

The journey of realization begins with a questing spirit. Seeking is an intellectual journey. If a person is sincere and one hundred per cent honest in his search, if there is no negativity in his thinking, if he is free from prejudices, if he has become a completely complex-free soul, attainment of maarifah for him is as certain as the dawn of light after the rising of the sun.

In the words of the Angel Gabriel, the Prophet of Islam once said:

> *"Worship God as if you were seeing Him." (Sahih al-Bukhari, Hadith No. 50)*

This is the most correct definition of ma'rifah. This may be put in a different way: God-realization is to have conviction in God's existence, as if you were seeing Him. How can one achieve this kind of ma'rifah? The way to achieve ma'rifah is to first of all discover creation and then, through creation, reach the Creator. For if there is creation, there must be a Creator.

In the first quarter of the 20th century, it was discovered that the universe had come into existence as a result of the Big Bang. This was like the discovery of God in the language of science. This means that when the universe has a beginning, then certainly there must be a beginner of the universe, who in religious terminology has been called God.

The conscious discovery of this God is known as maʿrifah. One who attains to this maʿrifah will experience an intellectual and spiritual explosion. He will believe in God through both reason and intuition, and it will be as if he is seeing God. He comes emotionally close to God. Such a discovery of God as revolutionizes one's personality is called maʿrifah. In the language of religion, this discovery is called maʿrifah, while in secular language it may be termed spirituality.

There is another necessary condition for the attainment of realization, and that is prayer (duʿa). Realization is a bilateral matter, in that a person's position is one of finding or receiving maʿrifah, while God is the giver of maʿrifah. An individual cannot receive realization without the help of God. All of one's efforts will remain fruitless unless God comes to his assistance. Prayer is not a mere repetition of certain words. Prayer is, in fact, another name for the heart's restlessness. Prayer is an external expression of an inner tempest. There is no religion without maʿrifah, and there is no maʿrifah without true prayer.

Wahiduddin Khan
New Delhi
March 20, 2011

Chapter 01

REALIZATION OF GOD

What is Maʿrifah?

Literally, Maʿrifah means realization. In religious terms, maʿrifah means man's realization of God, his Creator. He awakens in himself a profound consciousness of the reality of the creature and the Creator, and of the servant and the Lord. Maʿrifah is another name for conscious discovery. There is nothing mysterious about it. Maʿrifah of God means that man discovers God by deep pondering upon and contemplation of His signs, rather than by rumination upon His being. (al-Mufradāt fī Gharīb al-Qurʾān, al-Rāghib al-Iṣfahānī, p. 331).

This shows that maʿrifah relates not to knowledge alone but to reflection and deep thinking; yet, knowledge enables the individual to engage in deeper contemplation. When he focuses on maʿrifah, he engages himself zealously in the cognitive process of finding the Creator in His creation. As a result of this deep personal striving, he develops the personality of the realized soul. One who has achieved this kind of maʿrifah becomes an extremely serious person. He looks at everything with deeper insight. He starts introspecting intensely in his worship, behaviour, and in all his dealings. All these things begin to reflect this state of ma'rifah that he has achieved. He is able to converse with the angels. He is interested only in those things which elevate his thinking on ma'rifah. He now lives in the rarified environment of ma'rifah.

Ma'rifah—the Goal of Mankind

Scholars have defined ma'rifah as being man's first obligation. It would be more precise to say that ma'rifah is the purpose of life. The life before death is the beginning of ma'rifah, and the life after death is the culmination of ma'rifah. In the present world, a person receives God's ma'rifah in the sense of a preliminary discovery. In the world Hereafter, he will receive God's ma'rifah in the complete sense. The truth is that ma'rifah is an intellectual process, which begins in this present world and will continue eternally in the world Hereafter.

Chapter 51 of the Qur'an tells us that man and the jinns were created for the worship of God alone (51:56).

The purpose of this creation was that man and the jinns should be granted the sublime ability to achieve the realization of God in the highest degree. Therefore, on the one hand, the jinns and men were given the elevated intellectual capability required for this great purpose, while, on the other hand, they were given all the external resources necessary for them to carry out this task.

Ma'rifah literally means realization of something in the perfect sense. Ma'rifah, in other words, may be called intellectual discovery. This discovery does not relate to any short-lived familiarity with the truth but is rather another name for a long journey. The God that man is supposed to realize has such attributes as are alluded to in the Qur'an:

> *"If all the trees on earth were pens, and the sea [were]*
> *ink, with seven [more] seas added to it, the words of God*

would not be exhausted: for, truly, God is Almighty and Wise." (The Qur'an, 31:27)

The discovery of God who is so perfect, cannot be done in a short period of time. It is without doubt a journey which begins at a fixed point in time, but which is ultimately unending. The ma'rifah of God does not mean that with the help of meditation we shall have glimpses of God's being in the world of imagination. Moreover, ma'rifah is not ecstasy. Ma'rifah is an enhanced state of consciousness which can be achieved solely by contemplation of the divine creation. According to the Qur'an, Ma'rifah can be defined as a servant of God discovering God, the Lord of the worlds in all His Majesty and Glory to the extent that He becomes a centre of his love (The Qur'an, 2:165).

"And all his feelings of fear are associated with Him."
(The Qur'an, 9:18).

Love and fear are interconnected. When a servant of God engages in contemplation and discovers the Creator of the Universe in all His glory, in his heart he comes to acknowledge God to a limitless extent. Moreover, when he discovers the reality that the giver is God and that no one else can give anything to him, his heart becomes filled with the fear that if he is deprived of God's blessings, nowhere, on the earth or in heaven, will he find any other refuge.

"God has created man in the best of moulds." (The Qur'an, 95:4).

He has been granted all the intellectual capabilities by which he may achieve Ma'rifah of the Lord of the worlds. Beside this, in the external world that is nature, all those elements are hidden which may assist him in this journey. Now it is man's task to discover these elements of Ma'rifah in nature and experience such an elevated level of ma'rifa as will enable him to develop a divine personality.

Faith: Maʿrifah of God

Chapter 49 of the Qur'an addresses the believers thus:

> *"The Arabs of the desert say, 'We have believed.' Say to them, 'You have not believed yet; say rather, "We have submitted," for faith has not yet entered into your hearts."* (The Qur'an, 49:14)

And then another verse in chapter 5 of the Qur'an describes believers thus:

> *"When they listen to what has been sent down to the Messenger, you see their eyes overflowing with tears, because of the Truth they recognize. They say, 'Our Lord, we believe, so count us among those who bear witness. Why should we not believe in God and in the truth that has come down to us? We yearn for our Lord to admit us among the righteous.' And for their words God will reward them with Gardens through which rivers flow, wherein they shall abide forever. That is the reward of those who do good."* (The Qur'an, 5:83-85)

By studying both these verses, we learn what constitutes faith. Those fortunate souls who are recognized and accepted in the Hereafter by God will be ushered into Paradise, where they will live in a world of unending happiness and comforts.

The first thing that God desires is that faith should enter in one's heart (The Qur'an, 49:14). Just mouthing some words is not an act which will earn God's acceptance or which will establish the utterer of those words as a believer. Words which fall from the tongue are, in fact, only a verbal expression of the acceptance of faith.

To God, the truly desirable faith is that which so penetrates to the innermost recesses of one's heart, that it becomes the most important part of one's consciousness. It is from this that a person's spirituality begins to build.

From another verse, we learn that faith is another name for the realization of truth. That is, when man is truly able to realize faith and his Creator and is deeply aware of the fact that he is a helpless, powerless servant of God. When he reserves all greatness and all perfection for God, belief has so become a part and parcel of his personality that he surrenders himself before God. It is this deep experience of faith which is called ma'rifah or realization. Ma'rifah is the beginning of faith. Unless faith becomes a deep realization, it has no value in the eyes of God.

One sign of this realized faith is that when man experiences it, then his eyes overflow with tears. This experience produces tremors in his inner being. There is a great spiritual turmoil within him and his tears testify to this inner revolution. Any so-called realization of truth which is not testified to by his tears has no value in the eyes of God.

Such faith is no simple matter. In its reality, it is a universal acceptance of the truth. It is as it were to witness the divine reality before actually seeing it. It is to accept it voluntarily before the time comes when one shall have to accept it as a matter of compulsion. It is to bear witness to the All-Powerful God, testified to by the angels at every moment at the universal level.

Faith is, in fact, acceptance of the Hereafter as well as this world. It is to become more desirous of the blessings of the Hereafter than the blessings of this world. Those who proved to be desirous of this with all their hearts, minds and souls are the ones who will enter the eternal gardens of Paradise where they will reside without ever wanting to leave it. (The Qur'an, 18:108)

The Discovery of the Divine Words

What is realization, or ma'rifah? Realization is to recognize God in the unseen. That is, one is able to see God without actually seeing Him. Realization means, in fact, that man has psychological experiences of the presence of God.

Everything has a price. And the attainment of realization of God also has its price. This price is basically for man to tear down the element of doubt and see the higher reality. Only those can succeed in doing so who can save themselves from all kinds of distraction and apply themselves with total dedication to the attainment of realization. Everything which takes one away from the focus of attaining the highest reality, comes under the heading of distraction. This includes all kinds of negative feelings, for instance, hatred, bias, pride, the feeling of superiority and the following of desires, etc.

Man's mind has been given unlimited potential. It is not there for nothing. It is not meant to remain idle. It is for man to open up his mind and to discover the divine reality. According to the Qur'an the words of God are immeasurable (31:27). There is no limit to them. Similarly, the potential in the human mind is also unlimited. It is believed that the number of particles in the human mind are equal to all particles in the entire universe. Man has been granted this extraordinary capability so that he may use it to attain the Highest Reality—that is God.

The truth is that the favourite activity of the people of Paradise will be to keep eternally discovering the unlimited wonders of God. The present world is, in fact, for the purpose of preparing man for this unlimited activity in Paradise. The greatest happiness in Paradise is that of the attainment of realization. This journey to attain realization will eternally continue. Besides that, other material blessings in Paradise will be on account of God's magnanimity. (The Qur'an, 41:32)

High Levels of Ma'rifah

The Qur'an tells us that man was created so that he might worship God. In the words of the Qur'an,

> "I created the Jinn and mankind only so that they might worship Me." (The Qur'an, 51:56)

In this verse the worship of God means the realization of God. Discovery of the realization of God is without doubt the highest destination of anyone's intellectual progress. The noblest is he who can attain this level of realization. There are three kinds of such realization. The experience of realization of the first and second kinds has become a reality in history. So far as the realization of the third kind is concerned, the prospect of it becoming a reality has become achievable only in the 20th century for the first time in history.

The experience of the first kind of discovery was achieved by the prophets. This experience happened at the level of what is seen (ru'yat). It is described in the Qur'an in this verse:

> *"We showed Abraham our Kingdom of the heavens and the earth, so that he might have certainty of faith." (The Qur'an, 6:75)*

The words regarding the Prophet of Islam are similar.

> *"And certainly he saw him descend a second time." (The Qur'an, 53:13).*

This kind of realization is attainable at the level of the seen. This realization is reserved solely for the prophets.

The second level of realization is at the level of the discovery of one's helplessness. Man discovers his total helplessness as compared to the all powerfulness of Almighty God. In this way he achieves the realization of God. This has been aptly described in these words attributed to the 4th caliph 'Ali:

> *"I discovered my Lord by the shattering of my ambitions."*

The third kind of realization is at the voluntary or optional level. That is, man possessing total power, discovers the Majesty of God and voluntarily surrenders himself before Him. This is no doubt the most difficult thing to do. When the philosophers and the theologians engaged in such discussions as 'when God is almighty then man's position is only of total helplessness,' they concluded that the concept of man having power is only imaginary.

For the third kind of realization which is at the voluntary level, man had no previous point of reference by which he may understand this kind of realization. Therefore, he could not even imagine it. And what is not imaginable is not discoverable.

In present times the discovery of dark matter has for the first time given a point of reference in this regard. This discovery tells us that about 95% of space is filled with bright stars, but their brilliance is not visible, for the gravitational pull of black holes is so great that they are holding back their brightness and don't let it shine forth. This discovery is a divine demonstration. This demonstration in the form of a physical event tells us that for the powerful God it is also possible that He may withhold his Almighty power for some creatures. Therefore, to make human power real, God has temporarily withheld His power in relation to man. In spite of the absolute power of God, man has been given freedom in the real sense till Doomsday. This discovery is a reference point which makes possible the attainment of the third kind of realization. Now it has become possible that man may discover his helplessness. And afterwards with this point of reference (of black holes) he may discover that, despite his absolute helplessness, he may have total power or freedom for a limited period of time in this world. After this discovery what he has to do is to consciously surrender himself to God fully in spite of having total freedom. This is undoubtedly the most difficult thing to do. In this man has to live with two diametrically opposite things—on the one hand, total helplessness and on the other, total power. One who can develop his consciousness to the extent that he may live with two such opposites, is the person who can attain realization of this third kind. This realization is not impossible for man. Man naturally has this capability of being able to live as a mixture of opposites. This has been expressed by a western thinker, Walt Whitman, in these words: I am large enough to contain all these contradictions.

The Philosophical Concept of God

According to the concept of monism found in Aryan religions, God has no form. He is a formless God. That is, He has no independent being or existence. Everything which appears in this world is an expression of this God who has no being or no existence. This is indeed the philosophical concept of God. Philosophers generally conceptualize God in this sense. They use the word spirit, or idea, for God. This philosophical concept has become a part of the belief of the Aryan religions.

This concept of a non-existent God is entirely based on unjustifiable speculation. In the real sense, there is no basis to any argument to support this. The most significant point is that the universe that we experience in the form of creation does have a form in the full sense.

It would be illogical to say that God who was just a spirit, or idea, who had no Being, created such a diversity and multiplicity of forms. God is one who has the qualities or attributes of creation, and, in the spirit or idea, the quality of creation does not exist. Therefore, prima facie, this notion stands rejected.

In the world which has been discovered by science, everything is composed of atoms. Therefore, it is said that, in the study of science, we find the proof of oneness in the universe, that is, uniformity amidst exceptions in all material things. But this argument is not right. There is certainly a uniformity in material elements in the universe, and what has been created by the composition of these material elements. There is an extraordinary design in it, and design can only be a creation of the Mind. It cannot be a creation of some formless spirit.

The Heart and Mind

In ancient traditional times, the heart was regarded as the source of purification and realization ma'rifah. But modern scientific research has proved that the human heart is just a pumping organ which causes the blood to circulate. Ma'rifah and purification are, therefore, mind-based, rather than heart-based. Here the question arises about the significance of certain verses in the Qur'an which attribute ma'rifah and purification to the heart. The answer is that the Qur'an does not refer solely to heart; it repeatedly refers also to the mind: for instance,

> *"We have made it an Arabic Qur'an, so that you may understand." La'allakum ta'qilūn (43:3)*

> *"This is a blessed Book which we sent down to you (Muhammad) for people to ponder over its messages and for those with understanding to take heed." (38:29)*

And,

> *"... in this there are signs for men of understanding." (20:54) And, "...is there not in this strong evidence for a man of sense?" (89:5)*

The word used in these verses of the Qur'an is *'aql* (mind). This being so, the question arises as to how to explain these two differently worded sets of Qur'anic statements. In this case, according to the rules of grammar, one will be subordinated to the other. The way to apply this principle is to see in whose favour is the additional evidence, and then this additional evidence should be taken in its literal sense and the other will be subordinated to it. In this discussion of the heart and mind, there is additional evidence in favour of the mind, as discovered by modern science. That is why the verses which refer to the mind, will be taken in their literal sense, while the verses which refer to the heart will be taken in a purely figurative sense. In this way, both the words—"heart" and "mind"—as used in the Qur'an will be held to be synonymous.

There are some who hold that the heart has the capacity to think. That is, it is a thinking organ of the human body. But this is just a fallacy. Their claim is allegedly based on a physiological study which shows that there is a link between the heart and mind. But this claim is clearly fallacious. Of course, there is a kind of link between the mind and the other organs of the body. But this link is not a cognitive one. It exists only in a purely physical sense. The truth is that all the organs of the body act under the direction of the mind. None of the organs function independently of the mind.

The error of this argument lies in the fact that an ambiguous word, that is, communication, has been used to define this link. The right word to express this matter is direction, not communication. The difference between the two is that the act of direction is unilateral while the act of communication is bilateral. The word "direction" tells us that the mind unilaterally issues directions to the organs, whereas communication means that this activity between the mind and organs of the body is bilateral.

In the above argument, first of all the word "communication" was used for contact, then it was concluded that the heart was a thinking organ, whereas there is no scientific basis for such a supposition. The great loss occasioned by this error was that those who believed in the concept of heart-based God-realization were deprived of wisdom, for they were seeking wisdom in the heart, whereas wisdom did not stem from the heart at all. It is to compensate for this lack of wisdom that religionists (those who believe in one religion or the other) resort to concocted stories to make their point.

Man is a thinking animal. All of man's activities are controlled by thought. It is believed that man's personality is shaped by his thinking. It is this thinking faculty which is called the mind. These are the words— synonyms –for the mind that occur in the Qur'an: *Aql, Lub, Fuwad, Hijr, Nuha* and *qalb.* "Heart" is generally taken in the sense of a major organ of the body, but in addition to this, the word heart is also used in the sense of the mind (aql).

The most standard dictionary of Arabic *Lisān al-ʿArab* says that "heart" (qalb) is also used in the sense of 'the mind.' Farra Nahvi, a grammarian, corroborates this with an allusion to the thirty seventh verse of the fiftieth chapter of the Qur'an.

"There is truly a reminder in this for whoever has a heart, whoever listens attentively." (The Qur'an, 50:37)

In the Arabic language 'heart' is often used for 'mind'. For instance,

"You had no heart (on such and such occasion)." That is, you had no mind. (Lisān al-'Arab, Ibn Manzur, vol. 1. p. 687)

The truth is that the greatest thing man possesses is the mind. The words "heart" and "mind" are used synonymously with the only difference being that the word aql is used for "mind" in its literal sense, while the word 'heart' is used for the mind in a literary sense. In present times, it has been proved that the heart is only the centre of the circulation of the blood, while the mind alone is the centre of thinking. But due to literary usage, even today we use such an expression as wholeheartedly, and not whole-mindedly. This is true also for other languages.

The subject of the Qur'an is not anatomy: its subject is guidance to man. Guidance is totally related to reason and understanding. This being so, wherever the Qur'an uses the word "heart", in terms of the subject of the Qur'an, it is to be taken in the sense of mind or reason.

When the word "heart" (qalb) has two meanings, one as is generally understood in the sense of heart and the other in the sense of aql (mind) then in such a case the meaning of qalb (heart) used in the Qur'an, would be determined in relation to the subject of the Qur'an. In this case qalb in the sense of the heart will not be applicable. Qalb in the Qur'an will apply to the mind or reason. This is an accepted principle of grammar. This is applicable in both cases, in the Qur'an as well as in other literature. For instance, if a book written on the subject of anatomy uses the word "heart", then heart will be taken in the sense of an organ of the body and not mind.

On the contrary, when the Qur'an uses the word "heart", it will be taken in the sense of the mind. In every language one word often has several meanings. Each meaning is relative to its context. For instance, the word *dīn* in Arabic has several meanings. In chapter 1, verse 3, for example, the Qur'an has used it to mean the Day of Judgement, while in chapter 42, verse 13, the word dīn has been used in the sense of religion.

Purification of the Heart

Chapter 26 of the Qur'an tells us that only those will be held deserving of Paradise in the Hereafter who come to God with a sound heart. (26:89) In this verse, "heart" does not indicate an organ, in the physiological sense. It means rather the psyche.

Zahhak, the well known commentator has explained qalb ('sound heart') to mean 'pure heart'. Tafsīr al-Qurṭubī, vol. 13, pp. 114). That is, an uncorrupted heart. One who guards his nature of impurities, by successfully combating conditioning of his environment and thus succeeds in deconditioning his mind, will attain to God-realization. Such persons alone will be saved who come to God with a sound heart. (The Qur'an, 26:89)

The truth is that everyone is born with an upright nature. But when they fall under the influence of their environment, their nature systematically becomes tainted. To free oneself from external influences and restore one's nature to its original state, one must engage in introspection. This objective introspection guarantees that a man will return to having an upright nature or a sound heart.

> *"Those who reach God with a sound heart will be held deserving of being ushered into the eternal world of Paradise." (The Qur'an, 26:89)*

A sound heart or sound mind can be achieved by an intellectual struggle. One who engages himself in such a struggle becomes serious in the best sense of the word.

He develops the ability to discover the truth in a jungle of ideologies and conflicting information. He develops the ability to analyze all such information with total objectivity. He is able to look at things from the right angle. This is called having a sound heart or unimpaired judgement. This high level of ratiocination is achieved through great striving on a high intellectual plane.

Jihād Fillāh

In Chapter 29 of the Qur'an, there is a verse which says:

"We will surely guide in Our ways, those who strive hard for Our cause, God is surely with the righteous." (29:69).

In this verse, there are no such expressions as "Jihād fī sabīl Allāh" (jihād for the cause of God) but rather the word is "Jihād fillāh" (jihād in God). That is, there is striving hard not for the cause of God, but striving hard in God. Chapter 29 was revealed before the emigration to Abyssinia (5 A.H). That is why, it is clear that, in this verse the word jihad does not mean *qitāl*. Similarly, here 'jihād' cannot mean the practical following of divine commands, because no such word is used here. In this verse, what is attainable from jihad fillah is called guidance, that is why, in this verse, jihad fillah, would mean something which could be linked with guidance.

The fact is that, in this verse of the Qur'an, jihād means *jihād-e-fikrī*, meaning "thinking jihād" or "intellectual jihād", that is thinking about God, thinking *(tafakkur)*, reflection *(tadabbur)* about God, trying as much as possible to attain the realization of God, increasing one's faith through continuous study and observation.

Realization is the beginning of faith. It means trying to recognize God through the observation of His creation. By reading or studying the word of God, one can receive spiritual food from it continuously, thus converting one's daily experiences into divine insights. Observation of this kind is possible through total concentration, and such concentration is, of course, a great intellectual struggle.

"We will surely guide in Our ways", refers to the path of guidance. That is, the minds of the seekers of truth will open up more and more, new lines of thinking will develop, new aspects of realization of God will become clear to them. Just as God's being is unlimited, similarly, His realization is also unlimited. Those who strive hard to realize God through contemplation and observation will be fit to receive the blessing of this unlimited realization. This intellectual jihād has been called Jihād fillāh (jihad in God) in this verse.

Taking Lessons

When a person attains realization of truth, his thinking becomes God-oriented. It happens naturally then that he becomes a serious person. One aspect of this seriousness is characterized by the learning of lessons. A number of different words have been used in the Qur'an to express this. For instance, *tadhakkur* (39:9), *i'tibār* (23:21), *tawassum* (15:75), etc. Similarly, in the ḥadīth, too, we find such words, as the Prophet once observed:

> *"My silence should be the silence of thinking, my observation should be for learning lessons". Musnad al-Shihāb al-Quḍā'i, Ḥadīth No. 1159)*

The realization of faith or truth is, in itself, a thing of this nature. What is realization of faith? That is for man to discover the Creator by pondering upon His creation and finding the unseen world in the seen world. In the words of the Qur'an, he discovers inner realities through the signs of God. That is to say, over and above external vision he develops the capacity for insight.

Pondering or reflection or deep thinking becomes second nature for the believer. This is effectual everywhere. Having such a temperament makes him remember God continually. Every day, he discovers something which increases his conviction in faith, whereas other people see only the outward realities. The believer, due to his temperament, can see the realities beyond outward appearances. The processes of reflection and contemplation do not require a particular place or solitude. These processes continue at every moment in the minds of the believers. Even amidst a crowd he is engaged in deep thought. (The Qur'an, 24:37)

Learning lessons is spiritual food for a believer. For the believer, if material food is a source of physical strength, then learning lessons has the position of spiritual food. Without material food, the body cannot be healthy. Similarly, without intellectual food, spirituality cannot develop.

Intellectual Seclusion

I'tikāf is the Islamic practice of staying in the mosque for a certain number of days, devoting oneself to worship, and staying away from worldly affairs.

One kind of i'tikāf is that which is practised in the mosque during the month of Ramaḍān. This is mentioned in the Qur'an in the second chapter (2:187). The second kind of i'tikāf is what may be called intellectual seclusion.

According to a number of traditions, the Prophet of Islam (P.B.U.H) used to reflect most of the time. This is what is meant by intellectual seclusion, that is, deep thinking in silence.

I'tikāf of the mosque is of a limited period. On the contrary, intellectual seclusion is unlimited. The companions of the Prophet used to engage in intellectual seclusion. (*Shamā'il* al-Tirmidhī, ḥadīth No. 225) Some examples have been mentioned in Islamic literature. For instance, after the death of Abū al-Dardā' al-Anṣārī, someone asked his wife what special worship her husband engaged in. His wife, Umm al-Dardā', replied: Attafakkur wal itibar. That is, thinking and taking lessons. (Ḥilyat al-Awliyā', vol. 1, p. 208)

This intellectual seclusion is referred to in the Qur'an by these words: tafakkur, tadabbur, tazakkur, tawassum, ta'aqqul, etc. All these words mean thinking deeply on everything. This action of thinking is extremely important. It is by thinking that all noble qualities are produced, for instance, wisdom, realization, intellectual development, increase of faith, discovery of deeper meaning, etc.

This intellectual seclusion is extremely important for a believer, but there is one necessary condition for it, and that is to save oneself from all kinds of distractions. Without this, intellectual seclusion is just not possible. The truth is that, intellectual seclusion is another name for continuous intellectual activity. By this intellectual activity, we achieve what is called in the Qur'an, an increase of faith. (The Qur'an, 8:2) If there is no intellectual activity, there is no increase in faith.

The Intellectual Horizon

There are several planes upon which the intellect functions. We can say that there are many different levels. But higher truths can be experienced by only those individuals who have a high intellectual horizon. Those with a lower intellectual horizon cannot be acquainted with higher realities. The same is true of faith.

This is illustrated by the interactions of some of the companions of the Prophet, 'Umar ibn al-Khaṭṭāb (d. 23 AH), Mu'ādh ibn Jabal (d. 18 AH), and 'Abd Allāh ibn Rawāḥa al-Anṣārī (d. 8 AH). As recorded in the books of ḥadīth these men used to have conversations about God with one another and they would say that they were doing so in order to increase their faith.

> *Once 'Abd Allāh ibn Rawāḥa asked a companion to come and have faith for a moment. The companion who was with him became angry. He said: "Are we not believers?" Then in anger, the companion went to the Prophet and said:* "O Messenger of God, have not you seen how 'Abd Allāh ibn Rawāḥa wants to believe for a moment even after we have believed in you?" The Prophet replied: "May God have mercy on Ibn Rawāḥa, he likes such meetings as even angels envy." (*Musnad Aḥmad*, ḥadīth No. 13796)

Faith in God (*īmān bi-llāh*) or the initial stage of faith in God is attained after the recitation of the words of the *kalima*. But īmān is something which goes on growing. Therefore the Qur'an has likened īmān or faith to a plant which keeps growing.

> *"Do you not see how God compares a good word to a good tree? Its root is firm and its branches are in the sky, it yields its fruit each season with its Lord's permission."* (The Qur'an, 14:24-25)

When a believer thinks about God, when he studies this subject, when he observes the universe from this angle, throughout his contemplation, his faith in God keeps on increasing, he continues to discover God's high attributes and he keeps gaining in conviction again and again. Such are the believers who undergo the experience of īmān bi-llāh (faith in God) on a higher intellectual plane.

Levels of Realization

In ancient times, man could see only with the naked eye. At that time, man thought in a very limited way about the sky. By observation with the naked eye, it was calculated that there were not more than 5,000 small stars in the sky. But later, for the first time, in 1609, the Italian scientist Galileo (d. 1642), observed the sky through a telescope. Then, it was learnt that the stars of the sky were much greater in size as well as in numbers than had appeared to the naked eye. Galileo's telescope was a very small one at the early stage. Subsequently, there was a great deal of progress in this field.

A large telescope with a diameter of 200 inches was fixed in 1949, on Mount Palomar in California (USA). By means of this telescope, it became possible to observe the heavenly bodies of very large distance. Then, in 1990, the US developed the Hubble Telescope. It is a planetary telescope launched in space which constantly moved around 400 miles above the earth. It has a special type of telescope and camera. This system continuously sends the received information and images from space to the ground station. The Hubble Telescope has greatly increased man's knowledge of space. It is a matter of material observation. Just as there are different levels of human observation of the material world, there are also levels of God-realization, meaning that there are also different levels of man's realization of God. One should constantly strive to increase his level of realization. That way, there is no limit to God's splendour. Similarly, there is also no limit to the realization of God. It is according to the level of realization a person attains, that his status will be determined in the Hereafter in Paradise, neither less nor more than that.

Reflection and Contemplation: Sources of High Realization

Inevitably, a high level of realization is achieved only through elevated thinking. Regarding God's words and God's Creation, the more one thinks deeply, the more one will attain to deeper realization. The formula of ma'rifah is, in short—the more profound the thinking, the higher the degree of realization.

Many expressions have been used in the Qur'an to describe this deep thinking, for instance, tadabbur (reflection), tawassum (introspection) or ta'aqqul (reason). All these relate to different aspects of deep thinking, such as reflection, introspection, taking lessons, analysis, etc. In truth, everything in this world, whether great or small, has a source of thinking. If things are not taken in the simple sense, but rather, as subjects of reflection, then on reflecting with seriousness, everything becomes a source of realization. For instance, man walks on the earth daily but he does not think about it. If he thinks about it, this walking will become a treasure of ma'rifah.

Walking on the ground is apparently a simple thing, but, in reality, it is an extraordinary event. This incident of walking is a unique miracle of the Creator. This walking is possible only because of the diverse things which are coordinated in our support including the earth's gravity which gives us our balance and the pressure of the air all around our bodies. This pressure of the air is equal to 8 kilograms per square inch on our bodies, and this pressure on the whole body is about ten thousand kilograms. When man walks on the earth, oxygen is being continuously supplied, the sun in the vastness of space, brightens our paths. In this way, there are innumerable factors which directly or indirectly support us. Only with their help is it possible for man to walk on the earth and successfully reach his destination. There are many such factors in our world and when we reflect on all these things, it becomes the greatest means to the attainment of high ma'rifah or discovery of God.

Remembering God Often

I once penned an article entitled 'Realization—The Purpose of Humanity'. Almost immediately after it appeared in print, (Al-Risala, September 2010) a reader called to say: "I liked this article very much. Now I have a question: What is the definition of realization? How can a person be certain that he has achieved what in religion is called realization?"

My answer was that it had been defined in the Qur'an, with the injunction:

"Remember God often." (33:41).

Realization is actually the discovery of God. When someone has achieved the level of realization in the discovery of God, he experiences an elevated intellectual revolution. Now God alone becomes his primary concern. Such a person remembers God in the morning and in the evening, and, God being in his thoughts at all times, he enters into discussions about Him. This becomes the most obvious focus of his existence.

If a person finds something that he considers to be a very big thing, it is just human nature to talk too much about it. He gets so much pleasure in remembering that thing that he wants to think and talk about it all the time.

This is also true of the realization of God. When a person realizes God at the level of discovery, it takes possession of his mind. It is a natural desire if he thinks and speaks about it and even in seclusion he keeps reflecting on it. When a person is in this situation, it is proof that he has received the divine food which is said to be realization.

Intellectual Development

Intellectual development is undoubtedly the most important requirement of a human being. Through it, a man becomes perfect. Through it, a man succeeds in converting his potential into actuality. Through it, man elevates himself from the level of the animals and reaches the level of humanity. It is possible only through intellectual development that a man may become God's desired person in the real sense.

Intellectual development is not something new. This is exactly the same thing for which the phrase "increase in faith" has been used in the Qur'an (48:4). The beginning of belief starts with the discovery of truth. Reality is not a limited thing. There is no end to its vastness. Having faith means that man has started his journey into the realm of universal immeasurability. This journey continues, constantly marked by new discoveries. It has a beginning but it has no end. Increase in faith or intellectual development are two ways of describing this process. These differ in wording but in terms of their facts, they are one and the same. Faith can languish without ever-increasing journeys. But in the ongoing quest for truth, faith becomes a living thing.

When a person is born, very soon thereafter his physical development begins. This evolutionary process makes a child a full grown man. This is likewise true of intellectual development. Intellectual development also begins immediately after birth. But there is a difference between that and physical development. There is a known limit to physical development, but there is no known limit to intellectual development. Just as there is no limit to reality, there is no limit to intellectual development.

Reason and Human Nature Help in the Quest for Truth

The most important thing that every person needs is to achieve the realization of God, for there is nothing greater than this realization. In the acquisition of this realization, the parts played by reason and nature are equal. Neither of these two things is sufficient in itself for the acquisition of God-realization.

God-realization is a process, the first step of which is to go on the quest for truth. The course this takes is guided by reason, but reason in itself is not enough.

Reason or mind can lead a person only to probability. By rational thinking, one theoretically grasps the fact that God very probably exists. The next level is that of conviction, and the mind alone does not lead anyone to conviction. There is only one way to arrive at conviction and that is through one's nature. Every person receives his nature as a gift of birth. God has fully inculcated consciousness of Him in human nature, just as mother's love is innate in everyone. Through reason, man arrives at theoretical realization, and through his nature, man arrives, with certainty, at the realization of the truth.

A person's innate nature assists in the building up of conviction provided that he does not allow himself to succumb to different types of distractions. Distraction throws a veil over his true nature. In this way, his nature is not able to perform its real task. At present, causes of distraction have greatly increased, for instance, mobile phones, shopping, parties, family functions, business engagements, etc. Today, people are usually very far away from true realization of God. For them, God is just a formal belief, not a discovery. The reason for this is distraction. The price of realization is for a person to completely save himself from all kinds of distractions. Without paying this compulsory price, no one will be able to attain to the realization of God.

The Inner and Outer Aspects of Faith

There are two parts of the divine religion. One part of it may be called realization, and the other part obedience to commands. Although, both are equally important, just as soul and body are equally important for the human personality, there is a difference between realization and obedience to commands. That is, realization is central to the faith, unlike obedience of commands which is the relative part of the faith.

These two parts of religion have been mentioned in this ḥadīth in which the Prophet Muhammad said:

> *"Each verse of the Qur'an has an outer portion and an inner portion." (Ṣaḥīḥ Ibn Ḥibbān, ḥadīth No. 75)*

In other words, one aspect of the verse of the Qur'an is in its lines and its second aspect lies between the lines. In the light of this ḥadīth, the realization of faith is the name of the realization of religion while the commands of religion denote its external structure.

Let us examine the legal aspect of faith, which entails the recitation of these words:

> *"There is no god but God and the Prophet Muhammad is the messenger of God."*

One who utters these words has, according to religious law, become a believer but as far as the realization of faith is concerned, it does not depend just upon the recitation of such words. The realized faith can be achieved only through an intellectual revolution, and not just by mouthing some words.

The Meaningful Exception

There are many different things in the universe, without there being any uniformity in them. Indeed, in every part of it, there are exceptions. These phenomena in being exceptions are the proof that there is a great Creator of this universe. They are the proof of intelligent intervention, and intelligent intervention is the proof of an intelligent Creator.

For instance, the solar system is an exception in the vast universe. The planet earth is an exception in the solar system. The proportionate size of the earth is an exception. The rotation of the earth on its axis is an exception. The life support system on the earth is an exception. Life on earth is an exception, and so on.

These are the different exceptions that are found in our world, but they are not simply exceptions, but rather meaningful manifestations of divine instrumentality. They are proof of the fact that there is a God. He created this world according to His creation plan, He adopted the method of uniformity in things wherever He wanted and made some things distinctive and exceptional of other things wherever He wished.

For instance, there is uniformity in the structure of living bodies but along with this, every person has a different genetic make-up. The fingers of every person's hand are similar, but the thumb impression of each person is different. These exceptions in general are actually the proof of an intelligent creation and not the result of blind chance.

Universe without God Unexplainable

Albert Einstein is regarded as the greatest scientist of the 20th century. He was born in Germany in 1879 and died in the US in 1955. In 1921 he was awarded the Nobel Prize for Physics.

Albert Einstein made a profound study of the physical world. In his studies, he found that the universe had an extremely meaningful existence. Unlimited meaningfulness is immanent in every aspect of it. What is the source of this wisdom or meaningfulness which is inherent in the universe? Einstein discovered unlimited wisdom in the universe but he could not discover the Wise Being behind it. He exclaimed:

> *"The most beautiful experience we can have is the mysterious."*

Another saying of Albert Einstein is:

Why are scientists faced with this difficulty? It is because they have succeeded in discovering the meaningfulness of the universe, but have failed to discover the Creator of this meaningful system. That is why they wonder, when the meaningfulness of the universe is observable, why the Creator of this meaningfulness is unobservable. Where is the wise Creator? The truth is that without belief in God, the universe is rendered meaningless. It is belief in God alone that makes the meaningfulness of the universe understandable.

The Price of Finding God

A high level of realization of God is actually the greatest asset a person can have. It is, in fact, high realization of faith which makes it possible for a person to be different from animals. Achieving a high level of realization is just as possible as achieving anything else. The only condition is that one should pay its price. Without paying the necessary price, no one gets anything in this world and the same applies likewise to realization.

What is the price of a high level of realization? It is simply to make it the primary concern in your life and regard all other things as secondary. The man and woman who will pay this price will definitely reach the level of high realization. Those who do not pay this price will not be able to reach to this level regardless of how many good deeds they did.

The fact is that, repeatedly a person finds himself torn between two demands, the demands of faith and the demands of the world. On such occasions, if man ignores the demands of faith, and bows to worldly demands, even if he does this only once, such an attitude becomes the cause for his ruin. In this way, Satan gets the chance to stop man's journey of realization and push him backwards. This is the reality which has been mentioned thus in the Qur'an:

"When any evil suggestion from Satan touches those who

fear God, they are instantly alerted and become watchful;
but the followers of devils are led relentlessly into error by
them. They never desist." (7:201-202)

The reality is that, the journey of faith is a continuous journey. Even if a person stops for just a single day, his journey will be retarded for many years.

The Discovery of the Glory of God

When the famous American Boxer, Muhammad Ali (d. 2016) won the title of World Heavy Weight Champion, he said:

"I am the king of the world".

This is more or less the situation of every man and woman. Individuals are concerned only with their own glory. Nobody has discovered the glory of God.

The existence of the human being is a miracle of creation. A person should recognize his existence as an evidence of divine glory. But the condition of man is such that he sees only self glorification in his existence. He cannot discover the glory of God therein. This is actually the greatest tragedy of human history.

The famous French philosopher, Rene Descartes (d. 1650), is renowned for having said: "I think, therefore, I exist." This is a matter of self-discovery. But the most important thing is that a person must discover in his own existence the existence of God, so that he may say:

"I am, therefore, God exists."

This is the beginning of divine realization. The human being at first discovers the existence of God in the form of his own existence, after this discovery, endless doors of discovery open up for him. Every new discovery goes on increasing his realization and his awareness. Unlimited treasures of realization keep unfolding before him, until he reaches the highest level of conviction and realization of God.

The Journey of the Realization of God

When a government officer, without reason and without taking permission, fails to report for duty over a prolonged period, that is officially considered as a break in service and seriously affects the officer's seniority, even if he had already worked for twenty years in.

This is also true of the journey of the realization of God. If you start a journey of realization and for a long time continued to follow it, but then you make an excuse to temporarily stop this journey, this stop will not just be a temporary matter but will rather become equal to a break in realization, which means you shall have to go back to the point where you started your journey of realization of God.

Reality opens up to a person and then he goes on the journey of realization. But then on the way, some exigencies force him to stop his journey, for instance, family requirements, demands for materialistic advantages and the demand of personal matters, etc.

On such occasions, the traveller should not turn such types of demands into excuses for himself. He should continue the journey of realization by ignoring all other issues. One who does so will reach his destination while the man who made excuses about unnecessary demands will have a break in realization. This is a very serious matter. The voyager on his way towards truth must never make such a mistake, otherwise he will suffer such harm as can never ever be compensated for.

Deep Realization of God

Chapter 4 of the Qur'an has this to say:

> *"Believers, believe in God and His Message and in the Scripture He sent down to His Messenger." (4:136).*

Verse 14 of chapter 49 of the Qur'an offers a commentary on the authenticity of belief.

> *"The Arabs of the desert say, 'We have believed.' Say to them, 'You have not believed yet; say rather, We have*

submitted,' for faith has not yet entered into your hearts."
(49:14).

From this we learn that belief does not come about by the mere mouthing of words, you have to invite belief to enter your heart and then enshrine it therein. Belief should become a part and parcel of your whole personality just as dye becomes totally mixed into water. This is graphically expressed in chapter 2:

"Ours is the dye of God, and which dye can be better than God's." (2:138).

In another sense, this can be expressed as turning your belief into belief plus. That is, simple faith should be developed into a faith based on deep realization of God. In the Qur'an this has been called

"adding faith to your faith." (48:4)

That is, intensifying your faith. There are two ways of doing so: accepting the revelation of the verses and acknowledging what the signs in the universe indicate. We learn from the Qur'an that, for a true believer, pondering upon the verses revealed by God becomes a means of realization of the truth (5:83). Furthermore, according to the Qur'an, by pondering or reflecting on the signs scattered throughout the universe, it becomes clear that what the Qur'an has to say is the truth and that

"God encompasses all things." (41: 53).

From the study of the Qur'an and ḥadīth, we learn that there are two categories of faith, or the realization of truth—initial realization and high or sublime realization. In this respect, Paradise is also separated into two broad divisions (55:62). For those who have achieved a high degree of realization, they are alluded to thus:

"Those to the fore shall be the foremost." (56:10),

and for those who have a lower level of realization the words used are:

> *"Those on the Right, how fortunate are those on the Right!" (56:27).*

These are the two categories of the realization of truth. There is no other such category.

Faith: A Discovery of One's Relation with God

Hazrat Anas ibn Malik (d. 709) says that once a person came to the Prophet and asked him:

> *"O Prophet of God, which action is superior?" The Prophet replied, "Realization of God."3 The man again asked, "O Prophet of God, which action is superior?" The Prophet again replied, "Realization of God". Then that person said, "O Prophet of God, I am asking you about action and you are telling me about knowledge." The Prophet said, "A small action with knowledge benefits more, while a greater action with ignorance does not benefit at all." (Jāmiʿ Bayān al-ʿIlm wa-Faḍlihi, ḥadīth No. 214)*

In this tradition, by "knowledge" is meant realization of God. In this way, small or greater does not mean small or greater in quantity, but rather that action which is performed with God-realization, or inner spirit, is the true action. The action which is bereft of God-realization, or inner spirit, is of no value.

The truth is that Islam begins with the discovery of the existence of God and the discovery of one's relation with God. Another name for this discovery is faith in God. Whenever one receives this kind of faith, it necessarily begins to express itself in his life. One's thinking, one's speech, one's behaviour, one's worship, everything is a reflection or an expression of this discovery. The truth is that one's level of God's realization equals one's Islam, and the level of one's conscious discovery equals the level of one's external action.

God-realization is the spirit of Islam, it is the life of Islam. It makes one's Islam a living thing. The action done with God-realization is like a green tree, whereas any action without God-realization is like dried up wood.

Realization of God: Discovery of One's Helplessness

What is ma'rifah or realization of God? It is, in fact, a discovery of one's helplessness in relation to God. We must learn that God is Almighty and man exists in the state of total helplessness. When this discovery becomes a part of human thinking, penetrating to the innermost recesses of one's psyche is genuine realization. Once a devoted father wrote a letter to his dear son addressing him thus:

> *"O Moon, brightening the deepest recesses of my heart."*

When such sentiment is engendered in relation to the Lord of the World, this is true realization of God.

When you study the Qur'an and reach this verse:

> *"If all the trees on earth were pens, and the sea [were] ink, with seven [more] seas added to it, the words of God would not be exhausted." (31:27).*

While studying this in the Qur'an, your heart trembles with tempestuous feeling. You think that if God in His Omnipotence is at one extreme, man in his helplessness is at another extreme. At that time you exclaim with tears in your eyes:

> *"O God, just as Your attributes will never come to an end, so also will the words of God never be exhausted. In the same vein, my helplessness with respect to You is of an extreme degree."*

This is the ultimate extent of the discovery. It is on reaching this point that a person forms a picture of the final extent of his helplessness as compared to the omnipotence of God. This is the acme of human consciousness, the experience of which no creature other than a human being can ever experience. This is the point at which all the stars, planets, mountains and seas begin to envy man. This experience for any believer is like a very great and noble discovery. And another name for this superior discovery is ma'rifah. This superior form of realization can come to no one other than a human being in this vast universe.

The Purpose of Human Life

This verse of the Qur'an, 'I created the jinn and mankind only so that they might worship Me' (51:56) has been explained by 'Abd Allāh ibn 'Abbās, a companion of the Prophet of Islam, as meaning that 'worship' here means realization of God. That is, man has been created by God for His realization. The same has been expressed in a tradition, in these words:

> "I was a hidden treasure, I wished to be known, so I created Man." (Kashf al-Khafā', ḥadīth No. 2016).

The truth is that man's life is a journey of ma'rifah, from beginning to end. The initial part of this journey is spent in this present world, while the final and eternal part of it will be spent in the world Hereafter. Ma'rifah is an unlimited ocean. It is desired for a person that he be the voyager on this infinite intellectual and spiritual journey in the pre-death period as well as in the post-death period.

The Qur'an tells about the present world in these words:

> "He has given you all that you asked of Him." (14:34)

This means that the real purpose of a human being is to pursue the journey of God-realization, while for his material survival, he has been provided with all those things which are called the life support system. The life of the Hereafter is also, in fact, the life of ma'rifah. The journey of ma'rifah which primarily began in the life of this world, will also continue in the world of the Hereafter in its higher form. In the Hereafter, man will have the opportunity to see his Creator directly, to participate in His gatherings and to speak to Him. However, man will live as a guest of God in the Hereafter. Whatever man received in this world on the basis of need will likewise be given to him in the Hereafter on the basis of his desires and all his desires will thus be fulfilled. (The Qur'an, 41:31)

God-realization: A Personal Discovery

The Qur'an consists of more than six thousand verses, the longest of which is verse 282 in chapter 2. This verse concerns debt, and the necessity to put it down in writing, and it also gives commands in this regard in great detail.

The case of ma'rifah is treated quite differently, in that the Qur'an mentions ma'rifah but does not give any details of it. The root word of ma'rifah is 'arafa. Nearly seventy derivatives of ma'rifah appear in the Qur'an but details of it are not mentioned anywhere. For example, this verse of the Qur'an,

> *"When they listen to what has been sent down to the Messenger, you see their eyes overflowing with tears, because the truth they recognize," (5:83)*

shows only that a group of people heard the Qur'an and realized the truth it conveyed. But this statement in the Qur'an does not clarify exactly what this realization was which was attained by this group.

By comparing the above two verses of the Qur'an, a significant fact comes to light: God-realization is not some juristic issue which can be described in a specific language. God-realization is something that is achieved on the basis of self-discovery. This shall either be a self-discovered reality, or not be a discovery at all. For ma'rifah, God has chosen the same method for its seeker, as is called the discovery method in the field of education.

The truth is that ma'rifah is discovered by one through his own thinking and contemplation. In other words, ma'rifah is a creative subject rather than a traditional (taqlīdī) subject. To achieve God-realization, a creative mind is required. Maʿrifah or God-realization is achieved after a long intellectual struggle. It is self-discovery. Maʿrifah is not attained through any set, specific course, which one may learn from another human being through taqlīd, or the traditional way.

God-realization: A Creative Subject

There is no set course for attaining realization of God. It is not that one who begs for it will automatically achieve realization. Such thinking is a diminution of realization of God. The truth is that realization is a creative process. It takes an original mind to attain God-realization. Realization is a tempestuous experience. One achieves such realization through personal discovery. What is achieved through the utterance of ritual formulae may induce some kind of psychological state but it cannot be true God-realization. The realization of a God Who "manifests Himself in a new state every day" (55:29) cannot be had by blindly following any particular set course.

What is called creative thinking in secular terms is, in religious terms, called ijtihādī or creative thinking. Ijtihādī or creative thinking means discovering the hidden meaning in the statements of the Qurʾan. The discovery of such meaning is possible only through ijtihādī or creative thinking. This same thinking opens the door to an elevated realization of God.

The Qurʾan tells us that it has been revealed as a divine book, so that one may ponder over its verses. (38:29). This reflection based on such contemplation is the other name for God-realization. In the attainment of creative realization, the Qurʾan has the status of a book of guidance. The basic principle of realization has been laid down in the Qurʾan. To discover the hidden meaning by contemplation in consonance with this basic principle is a matter of individual judgement. The door of elevated realization opens through this creative process.

The Universe: A Source of God-realization

The Qur'an describes the power of God, in these words:

> *"When He decrees a thing, He need only say, 'Be!' and it is." (36:82)*

According to this Qur'anic verse, His power is so boundless that within moments He can bring anything into existence. But the history of creation proves that God did not take that course. According to modern scientific discoveries, the age of the present universe goes back fifteen billion years. God, first of all, made a composition of all the universal particles which came to be called the super-atom. An explosion, called the Big Bang took place in the super-atom and the condensed particles dispersed and spread into the vastness of space. These particles took the form of stars and planets. After this the solar system was formed, wherein the present earth was structured. Liquid water came into being after the mixture of two gases, hydrogen and oxygen. Then plants and animals came into existence. Finally, man was created and began to live on this earth.

If this entire phenomenon had taken place as a miracle of creation all of a sudden, it would have been only a cause of bewilderment for man and not any cause for contemplation. The Creator, instead of creating the universe in a short period of time, created it through a long process. Many factors were involved in the creation of the universe. In this way, it became possible for man to contemplate on the universe and discover the universal laws. With this, the universe became a source of eternal ma'rifah or God-realization for man. It became possible for a person to ponder day and night over the hidden creative process of the universe. Similarly, man may go on discovering the divine creative miracle without ever ending his journey of ma'rifah or God-realization.

Scientific Discoveries Provide Spiritual Food

Mentioning the "Words of God" (31:27) the Qur'an tells us that these words of God are so numerous that their enumeration would never cease.

What are these words of God? There is nothing mysterious about them. Rather, these refer to the mysteries of the universe. Modern science, in its reality, is another name for discovering these words of God.

The history of modern science is spread over 500 years. During this period, scientists have discovered many things in accordance with natural or physical laws. With the invention of the telescope and the microscope, the scope of discoveries has broadened greatly. The truth is that modern science in its nature, is the science of ma'rifah (God-realization). It has opened a great treasure of God-realization for the believers.

Here by science we mean popular science, and not technical science. On this subject, simple and easily understandable books are available in every language. The truth is that the greatest source of achieving ma'rifah is contemplation on the creation of God. Supporting data is always required for contemplation. Before the developments of science, very limited data were available on this subject. Now science has provided a huge library of unlimited data for the seekers of ma'rifah. Now, it has become possible for such seekers to pursue their journey endlessly. At every moment they may receive the spiritual food of ma'rifah. The process of spiritual development can go on within them continuously and never stop even for a single moment until the day they die.

God-realization: A Divine Gift

Man is in need of countless things, but he cannot create a single one of them. All these things are unilateral gifts from God to man. If God did not bless a person with these gifts, he would face utter ruination.

This is that aspect of human life from where the realization of God begins. When anyone consciously discovers what his exact position is, he becomes the recipient of divine blessing and inspiration. When such consciousness is developed within a person, a perfect bond is established with God, after which he continuously receives divine inspiration. In such a person, the process of God-realization starts taking place. If man for his part does not create any obstacle, the process of God-realization will progress continuously within him till it reaches its culmination.

Maʿrifah, in essence, is a divine gift. Any person, who receives this gift of maʿrifah will be deserving of the gift of Paradise. Maʿrifah is a worldly gift to the seeker by God, while Paradise is an eternal gift in the Hereafter.

The Qur'an tells us that the people of Paradise will be on the seats of truth (54:55). This shows that what makes a person most undeserving of Paradise is a lie, a direct lie or an indirect lie. Any person who refrains from all such types of lies will be deserving of entry into Paradise. God-realization makes a person, a man of truth and the truth becomes the means of taking a man to Paradise.

Learning Lessons from Mundane Occurrences

One quality of the godly person described in the Qur'an is the willingness to learn lessons (15:75). Learning lessons means recognizing some internal qualities from external signs. One who is able to learn lessons from things and experiences, can derive spiritual food therefrom. The ability to learn lessons is extremely necessary for the attainment of maʿrifah. One who does not have this capacity will certainly never attain to maʿrifah.

On one page of a 60-page magazine, published in 2010 by Australian Education International, a large- scale world map on the one hand shows India in white and on the other hand, at a distance of one thousand miles, it shows Australia in green. Indian youths are addressed in this Indian map with these words, "You are here." The caption on the map of Australia reads, "Your future is there."

On seeing this map, all of a sudden it comes to mind that man today is in a world prior to death, while his eternal future lies in the world after death. The present world is not one where one should be concerned with seeking one's future. The future lies rather in the world Hereafter which will come later. It is the intellectual acceptance of this fact which leads to the transformation of material events into spiritual experiences. We can learn lessons from everything in this world. If a man's mind is awakened, he will receive the nourishment of ma'rifah through his ability to learn lessons.

Reason-based Discovery of God

The source of the realization of God is, in the words of the Qur'an, reflection (tafakkur and tadabbur). (The Qur'an, 3:191) The attainment of God-realization by contemplation is entirely a function of the mind. In the human body, the act of thinking is done only by the brain. What is achieved by this process of thinking has been defined as God-realization.

In ancient times, there were groups of spiritual persons who held that the source of realization of God was the heart, and it was due to this concept that the method of meditation, by focusing on the heart became prevalent. But this concept does not relate to divine religion. This concept derived from the concept of monism. Those who believe in monism cherish the belief that God is in-dwelling. He is lodged in one's heart. But all these theories are based on supposition. There are no real arguments in support of them.

With reference to the heart, the Qur'an uses the word "understanding" (fiqh) (7:179), but this word "heart" is used only as a metaphor. It is not used in the actual physical sense. Those who have done research in the functioning of the heart have come to the conclusion that during the circulation of the blood there is communication between heart and mind. But this does not prove the theory of a thinking heart, because such communication takes place between all of the organs and the mind. According to modern medical studies what has been proved is that communication does take place between organs but that neither the heart nor any other organ besides the mind possesses the ability to think. The truth is that all the organs of the body are subservient to the brain, and in this, the heart is no exception.

Not Uncertainty

In the 9th verse of Chapter 6 of the Qur'an, a divine law is laid down on the matter of guidance. This is called the law of iltibās (doubt). This signifies that there is an element of doubt in everything. This law is for the purpose of putting man to the test. One who can tear off this veil of doubt will arrive at the truth and those who are unable to do so will remain in doubt—a state which is irremediable, because there are no alternative mitigating factors.

The same is true also of realization of God. One who is the traveller on this journey of realization, will face such types of situations again and again, when he will realize that he is in between doubt and conviction. He wants to believe in one thing, but along with this there are also certain factors which lead him towards doubt. He wants to believe, but he does not or cannot believe. People often face such hesitancy. This situation is the greatest obstacle to the attainment of realization.

When an individual becomes the victim of doubt or when he hesitates, there are two possibilities for him—on the one hand, on the basis of reason, he feels that the thing at issue is absolutely correct by scientific standards, but, fettered by his traditional mindset, he remains in doubt, feeling that he could be wrong. Despite being well educated and logically sound, beset by vague doubts, he remains in a state of uncertainty.

This condition of uncertainty cannot become an excuse for anyone. It is necessary for the seeker of God-realization to free himself from this state of hesitation. He must give importance to knowledge rather than to doubt. He must emerge from his state of uncertainty. He must accept proven realities. This is mandatory for the attainment of realization.

The Awakened Person

According to a tradition: "The world is a prison for a believer and a Paradise for the unbeliever." (*Ṣaḥīḥ Muslim*, ḥadīth No. 2956)

People generally take this tradition in a material sense, that is, the believer does not derive comfort from the material things of this world, whereas the unbeliever takes comfort from and derives happiness from material things. The reality is that the believer has to live according to divine laws, whereas the unbeliever is not bound by such laws.

But this tradition has another meaning which is in accordance with higher realization. When a believer completes that revolutionary process of discovering reality by which he attains higher realization, the world then becomes for him like a psychological prison, as if he had come into a world that was not created for him, and where he can find no spiritual solace.

When such a believer attains high realization, he feels that his existence has lost all relevance—for he has no words by which to express his spiritual discovery, he has no such audience as can understand what he has to say, he has no such environment as is fit for him to live in in his state of realization.

Such an awakened believer always feels as if he is in a balloon, where nothing is commensurate with his spiritual level. This elevated feeling is the certificate of entry into Paradise for all human beings. When God sees them in such a situation, He tells His angels to admit them to Paradise, because He had created Paradise for such people. Paradise is meant for such people and such people are destined for Paradise.

The Existence of God

The realization of God is an intellectual discovery. No one can achieve realization just by repeating God's name or, by meditation, training himself to silently utter the word of God spontaneously with every breath or beat of his heart. Such practices are irrelevant to attaining ma'rifah. They have no connection or relation with the realization of God.

There is a tradition which tells us that: "God has created man in His own image." (*Ṣaḥīḥ al-Bukhārī*, ḥadīth No. 6227) There is also an Arabic proverb which says: "One who has recognized himself, has recognized his

God also." (Ḥilyat al-Awliyā', vol. 10, p. 208)

This is doubtless very meaningful. It means that just as a human being has an 'I' (a sense of being), in the same way God has an 'I' on a much larger scale. The existence of this consciousness (the 'I') in human beings is an exception in the whole universe. While showing man's unique status, it also proves the existence of God. Because, if there is a small exception in this universe in the form of man, this is a sure proof of the existence of a very great exception: the existence of man necessarily offers proof of the existence of God.

This has likewise been expressed in the tradition—God has created man in His own image. That is, just as God has an exceptional existence, in the same way, human beings also have an exceptional existence in the universe. If a person ponders upon this exception, he will certainly discover God, he will call out—"I am, therefore, God is!"

The Virtue of Modesty

A *ḥadīth qudsī* is recorded in these words:

> *"God said: 'Pride is My Cloak and greatness is My robe, and one who competes with Me in respect of either of them, I shall cast into Hell.'" (Sunan Abū Dāwūd, ḥadīth No. 4090)*

This ḥadīth qudsī, meaning sacred narration attributed to God and relating to Him, teaches us the importance of modesty. The truth is that man's relation with God is established at the level of real modesty. If there is any sense of his own greatness in a person, this relation with God cannot be established. The true sign of real modesty is when one attains the state in which praise does not please him and criticism does not displease him.

One who is not truly modest, consciously or unconsciously, lives with a sense of his own greatness or importance. This kind of feeling is a veritable obstacle in establishing any relationship with God. The modest man, on the contrary, has the ability to fully accept divine inspiration. Whereas, where there is no modesty in the full sense, the immodest person, cannot be a recipient of divine inspiration.

The Godly Personality

According to a ḥadīth "Be alert through the wisdom of the believer, because a believer sees by the light of God." (*Sunan al-Tirmidhī*, ḥadīth No. 3127)

In this *ḥadīth* the wisdom of the believer means the wisdom of the realized person. It is a fact that one who has attained realization, becomes an unfettered person. He walks in the light of God, and no one has the power to extinguish the light of God.

One whose faith is at the level of ma'rifah to an extreme extent, becomes an aware person, in the sense that he experiences an intellectual awakening. He becomes a complex free soul. He develops the ability to discriminate between right and wrong (The Quran, 8:29). In this way his thinking becomes profound and he develops the ability to foresee things.

Realization of God endows the individual with the virtue of disinterestedness in worldly things. This is called *zuhd* (abstinence). It is a person of such virtue as has been described in a *ḥadīth* thus: "He is a servant of God, who has no interest in worldly things. God having planted wisdom in his heart, he speaks words of wisdom. God has shown him the evils of this world, and the remedy for them. God leads him in peace and security to Paradise, which is the home of Peace." (*Shu'ab al-Īmān*, al-Bayhaqī, ḥadīth No. 10050)

No Negative Thinking

It is recorded in a ḥadīth that you should not do tit for tat. That means that you should not mete out the same treatment to others that you receive from them. The course of action that you should take is that if anyone harms you, you should still do good to him. (*Sunan al-Tirmidhī*, ḥadīth no. 2007)

Realization of God is attainable by those men and women who always engage in positive thinking. But experience shows that in the present world it is not always possible to have favourable circumstances. In such a situation, there is only one formula for positive thinking. And that means being good to others whether their behaviour to you is good or bad.

Realization of God elevates only that heart which is totally free from negative thinking; such realization will never enter a heart which is not free of hatred, anger, and vengefulness. Man lives in a world where unpleasant experiences are commonplace. This is a law of nature. In such a situation, the only way for one who aspires to realization of God is to develop the ability to convert negative experiences into positive experiences, that is, he must continue to engage in positive thinking even in unpleasant situations. He has to develop the kind of high thinking which enables him to stave off the evil influences of the environment. This is the capacity which enables man to continue his journey of God-realization uninterruptedly.

The Discovery of the Existence of the Creator

The Prophet of Islam once observed: "God created man in His own image." (*Ṣaḥīḥ al-Bukhārī*, ḥadīth no. 6227). This means that man has been created as a natural exception in this vast universe. With his personal experience, man can understand that if a natural exception is possible here, then a supernatural exception is certainly possible. The existence of man, makes the existence of God understandable.

The vast universe consists of innumerable stars and planets. Our earth has countless animals, but no human-like creation exists anywhere in the entire universe. A human being is a rare exception in the entire universe. If we ponder over this, it is not difficult to believe that, similarly, a Great Rare Exception might also exist. This is to discover an unknown fact through a known fact. This argument is completely scientific and logical.

The famous French philosopher, Rene Descartes (1596–1650) said: "I think, therefore, I am."

The above-mentioned French philosopher, arrived at only a half-truth. He discovered himself, but he could not discover his Creator. Had he reflected further, he would have discovered the existence of God in the form of his own existence. His own existence would have become evidence for the existence of God. He would have discovered the Creator through the creation. He would have exclaimed:

"I am, therefore, God is."

Discovery of the Unseen God

John Stuart Mill (1806–1873), a British philosopher, writes in his autobiography (published in 1873) that he had formerly believed in God as a matter of tradition. But once his father, James Mill, said something to him which put an end to his belief in God. His father asked, "If God created man, who created God?"

Without doubt, the greatest hurdle in achieving God-realization is that, whereas God is limitless, man's mind has its limits. The matter of ma'rifah, in actual fact, is to attempt to discover a limitless Being by a limited being and to believe in Him with total conviction. This is ma'rifah. Without surmounting this hurdle, no one can be credited with attaining God-realization.

The discovery of God is different from other discoveries. For instance, gravity is also a subject of discovery, but this discovery relates only to science. On this basis, no one is going to receive eternal reward. The discovery of God, on the other hand, entitles the discoverer to a great reward. Those who have discovered God are destined to gain entry into Paradise.

That is why a price has been set on the discovery of God. Without paying this price, no one can be given credit for discovering God. This price is that, with his limited mind, man must encompass a limitless Being and, while engaging with the seen world, must be able to discover the unseen God. God-realization is the name of this discovery, and Paradise is its reward.

Silence and God-Realization

Traditions tell of how the Prophet of Islam usually observed silence (Musnad Aḥmad, ḥadīth no. 20810). Many traditions have been recorded on this subject. For example: "Hold fast to silence" (Sunan al-Dārimī, ḥadīth no. 2484). "A believer is one who either speaks good or remains silent" (Ṣaḥīḥ al-Bukhārī, ḥadīth no. 6018). "Anyone who observed silence, saved himself" (Musnad Aḥmad, ḥadīth no. 6481). "My silence should be contemplation" (Musnad al-Shihāb al-Quḍāʿī, ḥadīth no. 1159).

Observing silence means not only to remain quiet but also to contemplate. When a believer remains silent, he will ponder on his Lord. This is maʿrifah, or the discovery and realization of God. Silence is the door to maʿrifah. True silence leads man to true maʿrifah.

Silence gives man the opportunity to save himself from distractions. It brings greater clarity to his experiences and observations. He transforms ordinary facts into meaningful facts. He travels from the outer world to the inner world. He establishes his contact with God and His angels at the psychological level. All these factors strengthen man's God-realization.

Contemplation is the source of God-realization and without silence, the process of contemplation is not at all possible. Silence brings a person close to God. It provides the opportunity for him to achieve God-realization from the entire universe and this journey continues non-stop.

Discovery of God's Majesty

Muslim ibn Bashīr says that Abū Hurayrah wept during his illness. When asked as to what was making him weep, he replied:

"I don't weep for this world of yours. I weep rather for when I think that my journey is long and my provision is inadequate. And I feel I am on a hilltop which is going to heaven and hell and I don't know which way I will be led." (al-Ṭabaqāt al-Kubrā, Ibn Saʿd, vol. 4, p. 253)

These words of the Companion of the Prophet were an expression of a high level of realization of God. When man's realization intensifies, his state becomes like that of the above-mentioned Companion of the Prophet.

What is meant by a high realization of God? It is that state in which a person discovers God in all His Glory and Majesty. When a person so discovers God, in his eyes his own existence becomes insignificant in comparison to that of Paradise. He comes to regard his actions as valueless. He starts feeling that when he is presented before his Lord he will have nothing to offer. It is this feeling which makes him feel what is expressed by the words of Abū Hurayrah.

On the one hand, God being the most merciful, produces a feeling of hope in him but, on the other hand, when he sees how valueless his actions are, he starts feeling that he does not deserve to be rewarded. An insensitive person sees only his plus points while a sensitive person sees only his minus points. This is what separates the awakened soul from the unawakened soul.

Discovering God on Every Occasion

The fourth caliph of Islam, ʿAlī ibn Abī Ṭālib, said, "I recognized my Lord by failing to execute my will."

This is a simple formula of maʿrifah or God-realization. All men and women undergo such experiences daily when they realize that whatever they desired was not achieved. Sometimes this is a small experience and, sometimes a bigger one. Every such experience reminds a person of his limitations. Such experience tells man that he can desire, but the achievement of his desire is not in his control. Whenever any of a man's plans is unaccomplished, it reminds him of the reality that he has his limits.

Whenever man reaches his boundary, he should realize that immediately after this, the boundary of God starts; whether it is a small experience, for example, letting something fall from one's hand, or a bigger experience, like a plan or an idea not being fulfilled according to one's own desire. If a person is intellectually awakened, he will discover God on every such occasion, and it will become a source of ma'rifah for him.

This is the simple way in which one can derive food for God-realization on all occasions. Whether one is educated or uneducated, rich or poor, a degree-holder or a non-degree holder, one undergoes such experiences every day.

If a person awakens his mind and has the potential for contemplation, he will derive provision for ma'rifah or God-realization from every moment in his daily life. The fountain of ma'rifah will flow continuously in his heart and mind.

Uniqueness of a Human Being

The vast space consists of countless stars, planets, and galaxies. It has a solar system, with many planets in it. Among them is an exceptional planet which is called the earth. There are uncountable creations on this earth. Out of all this huge number of creations, only a human being has certain unique attributes.

In this vast universe, a man stands on this earth and speaks in human words, saying: "O God, You are the Lord of the Universe! I have acknowledged You with all Your Attributes and Greatness. I surrender myself to You with my entire existence."

These human words reverberate in space. They are heard by every form of creation. Then the entire universe calls out: "Look, this man is enviable. God was ingrained in our nature, but man has discovered God on his own. We praise the Lord without having the power of speech, while man speaks and praises the Lord with words. We are subservient by compulsion, while man has voluntarily surrendered himself. We established our relation with God at an unconscious level, while man has discovered Him at the conscious level and praises his Creator in words. We acknowledge the Creator in the state of the seen (mashhūd), while man has acknowledged God at an unseen level. We are worshiping God by imitation only, while man worships God in a creative way. We demonstrate the greatness of God in unspoken words, while man expresses this by the power of speech. We praise our Lord in a limited way, while man praises God on an unlimited scale."

This is a higher form of God-realization. Conscious God-realization of this kind can be attained only by a human being. These are the people of a higher level of ma'rifah, who will be ushered into Paradise.

God and Paradise

Man is unique in having two faculties bestowed upon him—one, the faculty of thinking and the other, the faculty of enjoyment. If man utilizes both these faculties in a proper way, he will, on the one hand, discover the existence of God and, on the other, the existence of Paradise.

The phenomenon of thinking is an exceptional human attribute. The well-known French philosopher René Descartes observed:

"I think, therefore, I am."

Similarly, we can say that the existence of the small thinker is a proof of the existence of the Big Thinker.

The same is true of the sense of pleasure. On reflection, man should realize that his is a unique existence in the universe, exceptionally gifted as he is with the sense of pleasure.

The discovery of this reality is in itself a discovery of a greater reality. If a sense of pleasure exists in this world, then certainly the resources for its fulfilment must also be present because, in this world, there is a pair for the completion or fulfillment of everything. According to this general law of nature, there should certainly be present a pair for the sense of pleasure as well; that is, fulfilment too should be possible in this world. This phenomenon is convincing evidence of the existence of Paradise.

Self-Negation: A Means of Discovering God

Everything has its price. Without paying the price one cannot receive the things one desires. Similarly, realization of God also has its price, and this price is man's own being. Nothing less than that can be the price of realization of God. This is something that can be attained only at the cost of the negation of one's own self. If one is not willing to negate oneself, one cannot achieve realization of God.

One's own negation does not mean some kind of mysterious words counted out on the rosary. This can be done only through reflection and contemplation rather than by doing physical exercises in the name of spirituality. What is self-negation? Self-negation for man is to discover the Lord to the extent that his own existence in comparison to that of God becomes totally valueless.

Self-negation is achieved by developing such qualities as modesty, humility, acknowledgement, introspection, selflessness, simplicity, being God-fearing, having fear of Hell, and the desire for Paradise. These qualities cannot be produced by spiritual exercises; they can be produced only by a profound thinking process. This action of self-negation begins with the deep discovery of the divine truths and this continues till the last breath. Self-negation is in fact another name for the discovery of reality.

In reality, man is nothing. For him even an ordinary accident becomes unbearable. He cannot have any knowledge of anything with conviction.

Man at all times is in need of external resources. Any part of man's being (e.g., some major organs) can stop functioning. Man knows neither the reality of life nor the reality of death. Man desires many things but he has no power over anything. Man is apparently free, but except for exerting his own will he has no freedom to control factors outside of him.

Another name for the consciousness of these aspects of human existence is self-negation, and it is this self-negation which is the greatest means of attaining realization of God. In one respect, self-negation means discovering God the Almighty and, in another respect, it means discovering oneself as a totally helpless creature.

Making the Discovery of God One's Personal Interest

Realization of God is unrelated to any romantic love for God. It relates to the deeper feeling in a person that his future depends solely on one God. He can have his beloved Paradise only when God gives it to him.

Similarly, one can save oneself from the dreaded Hell only when God saves him. It is only when this kind of deep consciousness develops in one that the door to realization of God opens to him.

Realization of God is no philosophic concept. Ma'rifah is inevitably linked with personal interest. The attainment of a high level of such realization is possible only when man discovers it at an intellectual level; when he learns ideologically that nothing save this can be his real destination; when a person's mind is fully convinced of its veracity.

On the other hand, it is also essential that a person's personal interest should be fully associated with the realization of God. In this matter he should develop a heightened sense of discovery to the extent that he starts feeling with great intensity that without the attainment of God's realization his existence will be rendered meaningless, his life will become desolate, all his future prospects will be set at naught, and he will be a failure in every respect.

Only when this is an individual's thinking, both theoretically or ideologically and practically in all respects, does he become desirous of God-realization to the last extent that all the doors to it are opened immediately to him. No door remains closed to him. This is the way of God-realization. It is not possible to reach the goal of God-realization by any other path.

Uncertainty about Oneself

It is only when a person has the feeling that of all human beings he is the only one who has attained a high level of God-realization or that of all people he is the only one who is deprived of a high level of God-realization that he can actually reach a high level of God-realization. Yet no one can say with conviction that he has attained a high level of God-realization.

The reason for this uncertainty is that God-realization is not the name of any external course by which one might think that one has learned all that is possible for him to learn and that one has now attained God-realization. It is wholly an internal state, and giving any verdict about an internal state is possible only for God, the Lord of the world.

Anyone who is a seeker of God-realization cannot himself come to any such conclusion. The high level of God-realization is, in fact, another name for the sublime discovery of divinity. Whenever God's servant reaches this high level, he feels that, in comparison to God, his position is zero. God is everything and he is nothing.

This discovery tells him that in this matter the entire power of decision-making is in the hands of God. Man has no say in this matter. This discovery demonstrates that the entire matter is wholly unilateral.

Who are the people who may be said to have attained God-realization? They are those whose realization is confirmed by God. And God's decision will be made known only on the Day of Judgement and not even a second prior to that Day. This is why one who has done everything to achieve God-realization still has a feeling of uncertainty about it till the very last minute.

An Obstacle in the Path of God-realization

A certain American scholar having studied Islam, once wrote a book on the subject in which he observed that the greatest concern of Islam was Allah.

This is one hundred percent true. The door to realization is open only for one who makes the one God his sole concern. This being so, the greatest obstacle in the path of realization is man's failure to make God his sole concern. As far as the realization of God is concerned this is undoubtedly the most important thing.

In essence, one who makes something his sole concern never allows his attention to deviate from that thing. He goes to bed thinking about it and he gets up in the morning thinking the same thoughts. That thing so dominates his mind that almost all other things get eliminated from his consciousness. Man thinks on that same topic. He speaks with others on that same topic. He reads about that same topic and he has discussions about that same topic, to this extent that his heart and mind find solace only by delving further into that same topic. He thinks of it both when he is alone and when he is in public; he does not fail to mention it whatever the occasion.

This is what it means to make something one's sole concern. The person who makes God his sole concern is destined to experience the realization of God. One who is not able to make God his sole concern will certainly never attain to the realization of God. It does not matter whether or not he repeats God's name on the beads of his rosary. The real obstacle to the attainment of realization is man's holding something else to be greater than God. Considering someone greater is sometimes done consciously and sometimes unconsciously, but the result is the same, that is, failure to arrive at the high realization of God. Any man or woman who desires to have an elevated realization of God shall have to pay this price of diverting his or her attention away from all other things and making the one God his or her only concern. In reality, it is a psychological sacrifice. Only one who is capable of making this sacrifice shall receive that divine blessing which is known as ma'rifah, or realization.

The Natural World Leads to God

The universe is a great library of ma'rifah or God-realization. Everything in the universe speaks of God-realization. This manifests itself in the form of the law of nature throughout the universe. If a person ponders over creation, he will find that every aspect of the universe is giving the lessons of God-realization.

The sun symbolically displays that ma'rifah or God-realization is that which enlightens the existence of man from the inner self to the outer self. The flowing river tells man to achieve God-realization in such a way that it flows as a spring in the soul. The lush green branches of a tree when swayed by wind convey the message to man to achieve God-realization in such a way that it becomes a thrilling experience for him. The chirping of birds tells man that discovering the wonders of God should happen in such a way that praises of God flow from his tongue. The greatness of the mountains silently expresses the discovering of God in all His greatness, and so on. The same is true of the entire universe. Everything in the universe sends out the message of God-realization in natural terms as if the entire universe is a great library of God-realization. In the same way that a scholar enters the library and derives knowledge from books, a true human being receives the intellectual food of God-realization from the divine library of the universe. The library of the universe is an unlimited treasure of ma'rifah. Every particle of the universe has the status of an encyclopedia of ma'rifah. Here the leaf of a tree enshrines a library of God-realization within it. This has been expressed thus by a Persian poet: Barg Darakhtan-e-sabz, dar nazar-e-hoshiar, har waraqe daftare ast marifat-e-kardgar. (The leaves of the green tree, to a wise man, serve as a great resource of the realization of the Creator.)

Ma'rifah: A Life with God

There is an Arabic proverb, "I do not know is half of knowledge," that is, knowing our own unawareness is the starting point of knowledge. When a person learns that he does not know, the spirit of knowing is awakened within him. This spirit finally leads him to knowledge, and his unawareness becomes awareness. The same is true of ma'rifah. Man must first of all discover that he lacks in ma'rifah, and only then will the search for ma'rifah begin within him and will finally bring him to ma'rifah. What brings one to knowledge is the spirit of enquiry. This spirit is a must for ma'rifah. Man must first of all know that without ma'rifah, he is in the dark. With ma'rifah, it is like living in the light, while without ma'rifah is like living in darkness. Without ma'rifah, man can only experience failure, in this world as well as in the Hereafter.

Ma'rifah enables man to live on a higher plane. A man of ma'rifah is able to understand the realities as they are. Ma'rifah makes a man worthy of being in the company of angels. Ma'rifah enables man to receive divine inspiration. Ma'rifah makes a man perfect. Ma'rifah is the source of guidance in this world and the source of Paradise in the Hereafter. Ma'rifah is the right beginning for a human being's journey in life. Ma'rifah is a means of leading an unaware man to a life of awareness. Ma'rifah enables man to lead a life with God rather than a life without God. It is possible with ma'rifah for man to discover his high potential and, with the help of God, make it an actuality. Ma'rifah enriches knowledge to the maximum and leads to the perfection of life.

Positivity: The Fertile Ground of Ma ' rifah

For a plant to grow, fertile land is essential. Only on fertile land will it be possible for a plant to grow into a green tree. Such a development cannot take place on barren land. For a tree to grow, fertile land is indispensable. Fertile land is favourable for the plant, while barren land is totally unproductive. The same is true of ma'rifah. Ma'rifah can take place only in such a seeker as has a noble personality. One who is not such a seeker cannot attain to ma'rifah. He has to have a positive personality. Conversely an unfavourable personality may be described as a negative personality. One who desires that the orchard of ma'rifah should grow within him should turn himself into a positive personality, whatever the cost.

A man with a negative personality is one who is of a reactionary disposition. He is one who succumbs to the influence of his environment. Because of his immature consciousness, he is easily influenced by external events. Such a person who is of a negative bent of mind can never receive the blessing of ma'rifah. One with a positive personality, because of his mature consciousness, is able to rise above external circumstances, and is able to form his opinions uninfluenced by external pressures.

He will ultimately convert negative experiences into positive lessons. By the grace of God, one endowed with a positive personality finds the opportunity to think along the right lines, and continues to discover ma'rifah so that the process of building a spiritual personality is ever ongoing. The attainment of ma'rifah is possible only on the basis of a positive personality.

The Light of God-realization

A tube light in your office with no connection to the powerhouse will never shine. But the moment it is connected to the powerhouse, it lights up. This material event is analogous to the spiritual reality which is called God-realization. If there is no contact between God and man, his existence will be devoid of God-realization. But when there is a connection between God and man, immediately, the heart and mind of a person is illuminated with the light of God-realization. According to the Creation Plan of God, man's position in this world is that of a taker, whereas, the position of God is that of the Giver. Man in every respect is a needy creature. He cannot fulfil any of his own wants: it is only God who fulfils his every requirement. This aspect of man's personality makes him feel helpless all the time. This feeling of want is an integral part of a man's personality.

Anyone who is consciously aware of this lacking will become a seeker, while one who is not aware of this short-coming will always be suffering from a feeling of deprivation. God-realization or ma'rifah is the answer to this want in a person, something he is born with. Nothing other than God-realization can ever fulfil this lacking in man. Just as a bulb does not light up without being connected to the power house, a man's life without ma'rifah remains unlighted, and nothing else can bring him enlightenment.

The Living Discovery of God

A Western commentator writes—"Every day when in the early

morning the first ray of sunlight peeps into your room jump out of bed and say: 'Wonderful! What a bright new sun!'" The realization of God Who is the Creator of sun, is without doubt, countless times greater than that of the sun. One who has discovered God, will discover God's splendour every morning and evening, his realization of God will become an endless journey of divine light. Ma'rifah is not something inert like a piece of stone, ma'rifah is a growing thing like a plant. A tiny seed grows and grows until it develops into a tall green tree. The same is true of ma'rifah.

The beginning of ma'rifah is from the acceptance of faith. Afterwards, through study and contemplation, this acceptance of belief keeps on growing until it becomes a full green tree of ma'rifah, rather it becomes a full orchard of ma'rifah. This development or growth of ma'rifah continues and does not end till one's death. Ma'rifah is another name of the discovery of the wonders of God. God's wonders are countless, therefore the ma'rifah of God is also an unending journey. This journey continues eternally through new discoveries. Death is not an end to this journey. After death the believer's journey of ma'rifah will continue with much greater speed. The truth is that the most pleasant experience of the people of Paradise would be to live in the garden of ma'rifah, to breathe in the air of ma'rifah. This would indeed be the greatest and most pleasant gift of Paradise.

The Difference between Ecstasy and God-realization

Ecstasy and realization appear to be similar in meaning but, in reality, they are quite different from one another. Ma'rifah, or the realization of God, is a noble Islamic quality, whereas ecstasy is not related to Islam. Anyone may have this experience of ecstasy. But the truth is that ecstasy has nothing to do with religion. Even music and dance can bring about a state of ecstasy in a human being.

Ma'rifah relates to conscious discovery. When a person engages in contemplation and discovers his Creator, then at the intellectual level he discovers something spiritual (rabbānī). This is called ma'rifah. Ma'rifah, in other words, can be called intellectual development. If intellectual development takes place in a purely natural way, it will inevitably take a person to the discovery of his Creator, and the conscious discovery of the Creator is another name for ma'rifah.

Ecstasy, on the contrary, is not something that takes shape on a conscious plane. It is a feeling or state. Such feelings can be produced by many things. They could be religious or non-religious in nature. Ma'rifah, on the other hand, awakens the capacity for deep thinking and contemplation in the person concerned, whereas ecstasy only causes one to enter a trance-like state. Temporarily, a person feels himself in a tension-free state. A trance can give one a vague kind of thrill, but it cannot produce intellectual and spiritual development.

Ma'rifah brings about an intellectual awakening in the believer and brings him nearer to his Lord, whereas a trance makes it possible for a person to be lost in himself, unable to perceive the external reality. Ma'rifah increases insight, whereas a trance only leaves one in a state of unawareness. Ma'rifah is a conscious state, whereas a trance only produces a thrill.

Realization and Prayer

Prayer (du'ā') is a natural utterance for one who has a spiritual bent of mind. But without realization prayer is only a repetition of words. The prayer that comes from a realized soul is prayer in the real sense. The prayer that is devoid of ma'rifah is little but lip service; it has no value. Prayer is a form of worship, and the real form of worship is one of which realization of God is an integral part.

Prayer is of two kinds. One is that which requests God to fulfill some need of the supplicant with reference to some personal problem he is facing and entreating God to provide a solution. For instance, one who is jobless prays to God to help him get a job. This is a common form of prayer. This prayer is rewarded according to the suppliant's sincerity. It depends upon God whether, after hearing such a prayer, He fulfills it there and then or postpones it until later.

Another form of prayer is that in which the person praying projects his problem as the problem of God Himself. For instance, in ancient Spain, at a time when there had been a drought, the Muslim king, Sultan ʿAbd al-Raḥmān al-Nāṣir (d. 961 CE), said in his prayer to God:

> *"This forehead of mine is in Your hands. Will you punish people because of me? You are the Ruler of all rulers (of earth). Nothing of mine lies hidden from You." (Tārīkh al-Islām, al-Dhahabī, vol. 25, p. 444).*

In this prayer during the drought, the rains were held to be a matter of God's own mercy rather than the solution to the demands of man's needs. The implication of this is that God, being the most merciful of all, would not punish people if it were not their fault.

The first kind of prayer is uttered owing to human needs. But the second kind of prayer comes from the heart of a person with deep God-realization. The second kind of prayer is the result of the discovery of God at the level of realization. This kind of prayer comes out of the heart or mind of a person only when he has some special experience of God's nearness. There are many instances of this kind of prayer in the books of Hadith.

The Discovery of One's Ignorance

The journey of realization of God begins with lā ilāha (there is no god) and then finishes with illā Allāh (but God). The individual must first become a seeker and later become a finder. It is this order of the journey of maʿrifah that applies to common man as well as to a prophet.

There is a saying in the Arabic language:

lā adrī niṣf al-ʿilm (saying "I don't know" is half of knowledge).

First an individual has to discover his own ignorance, and then a spirit of enquiry is born within him. The greater his acknowledgement of his own ignorance, the greater his spiritual and intellectual learning. It is a natural reality to which there is no exception.

Maʿrifah, or the discovery of God, is not something to be inherited such that a father may give it to a son and the grandson may receive it from his forebears. Maʿrifah is ultimately something of a personal nature. Whenever anyone attains God's realization, it will happen only as a result of personal effort. Without personal effort, no one can ever achieve maʿrifah. Whatever a person receives without personal struggle will be just a kind of traditional belief rather than a living maʿrifah.

Maʿrifah relates to the entire personality of the human being. Maʿrifah initially is achieved at an intellectual level. Subsequently, through a natural process, it pervades his whole personality. The attainment of maʿrifah for anyone colors his whole personality in its hue. No aspect of his life will remain unaffected by its influence.

The journey of maʿrifah is indeed one of discovery. This discovery continues throughout one's life. One who thinks that he has achieved perfect maʿrifah would, in effect, never have discovered maʿrifah at all.

Make God Your Supreme Concern

Most people talk frequently of maʿrifah without ever having attained it. The reason is that they want maʿrifah but are not willing to pay the price for it, and in this world nothing can be achieved without paying the price. What man ought to do is that when he is not ready to pay the price for something, he should not talk about it. Talking about something for which he is not willing to pay the price means that he is only mouthing words about maʿrifah without understanding its significance.

There is a saying in Arabic:

"Knowledge gives you a part of it only when you give yourself to it completely." (Al-Faqīh wa'l-Mutafaqqih, al-Khaṭīb al-Baghdādī, vol. 2, p. 204).

This is true of maʿrifah. The price of maʿrifah is that a person should give his all to it, make it his sole concern, think of maʿrifah while going to bed, and think of maʿrifah while getting out of bed. He should engross himself in it to the point of dreaming about it. The price of maʿrifah is total surrender. One who does not totally surrender to maʿrifah will find that the doors of maʿrifah will never be opened to him.

The Form and Spirit of Religion

There are two aspects of the knowledge of religion—one is the knowledge of the form (masā'il) of religion, and the other is the knowledge of the maʿrifah of religion. Commands or laws relate to the form of religion, whereas maʿrifah is related to the spirit of religion. To become religious, both are essential. Knowledge of the commands and laws does not give man knowledge of maʿrifah, but if one acquires knowledge of maʿrifah, he will certainly grasp the commands of religion. The journey of religion begins from maʿrifah and arrives at the commands and the laws. On the contrary, knowledge of the commands does not automatically lead one to maʿrifah.

What is maʿrifah? Maʿrifah, in fact, is man coming to discover the reality of life, finding the answer to his internal quest, and the right ideology of life. Maʿrifah, in a word, is internal revolution. When this internal revolution is experienced by someone, his whole personality is transformed—his thinking, his speech, his behavior, his ambitions, his desires, his outlook on things, and his criterion for accepting or rejecting something. All things, in short, are colored by the hue of God.

After the acquisition of maʿrifah, the personality of the believer manifests itself in different ways. One of these manifestations is in the form of worship. Divine commands relate to one of these manifestations. Such manifestations are essentially produced by internal change.

The role of commands is to define the right limits of these manifestations. The task of a reformer is to place the utmost emphasis on producing the inner spirit—that is, ma'rifah. This is the natural method of reform. On the contrary, if only commands or laws are emphasized, this amounts to a shift of focus. With such a change, no desired result can be produced. In that case, religion will become entirely based on laws, whereas religion should be based on ma'rifah.

Chapter 02

PURIFICATION OF THE SELF

Purification of the Self (Tazkiyah)

The Quran mentions four responsibilities of the Prophet, one being the purification of the self (Qur'an 2:129). The fact that this is set forth in the scriptures underlines the importance of purification. It is, therefore, essential for believers to give first priority to the purification of the self in their lives. Similarly, it is necessary for the preacher and the reformer to attach great importance to the process of purification.

Purification (Tazkiyah) covers a number of imperatives: purifying oneself of the temptations of the self and Satan; refraining from negative reaction when faced with unpleasant experiences occasioned by others; and remaining resistant to such influences as cause one to deviate from the straight path.

The truth is that man has been created by God with an upright nature. But in the life of this world, it repeatedly happens that external factors compromise this positive aspect of his character. A person ought to become aware that this is an ever-present possibility and should make unremitting efforts to ward off undesirable influences.

The task of the Prophet was always to make people aware of this principle of purification and lead them towards attaining it. In this context he should be looked upon by mankind as a unique model of self-purification.

With his contemporaries, the Prophet's approach to this task of tazkiyah was direct. For later generations the performance of the Prophet's task has to be continued indirectly. On the subject of self-purification, complete records of the Prophet's sayings and deeds, and the sayings and deeds of the Prophet's Companions, have been preserved in the books of sira (the Prophet's biography), and later generations should feel themselves duty-bound to seek guidance from these records. Those who can read can do so directly, while those who cannot read themselves may seek the assistance of religious scholars, so that they can adopt that course in their lives.

The Continual Growth of One's Personality

As stated in the second chapter of the Qur'an, one of the duties of the Prophet vis-à-vis his contemporaries was

> *"to teach them the Scripture and wisdom, and purify them" (Qur'an 2:129).*

It is necessary for every believer to purify himself. Without purification, that calibre of personality, which is called in the Qur'an a God-oriented personality (Qur'an 3:79), cannot be developed. The truth is that purification alone can lead one to heaven (Qur'an 20:76). Tazkiyah literally means growth, one example of which can be seen in the tree. A tree is the result of the growth of a seed. When a seed finds a favourable environment, it starts growing until it becomes a green, verdant tree. The same is true of the purification of a human being. In this sense, tazkiyah also covers intellectual development.

God has created a person with great potential, and this potential of the human personality is actualized by tazkiyah. In this sense it would be right to call it the building of the human personality on a divine foundation. When a person discovers and realizes faith, he has in actual fact started the journey of tazkiyah. Gradually, he becomes a purified soul, or an intellectually and spiritually developed personality. This is the person who will gain entrance into the eternal Paradise of the Hereafter. There is nothing mysterious about tazkiyah. Tazkiyah can be attained not through meditation but through contemplation and reflection. This entails pondering over or thinking about oneself and the universe, and receiving intellectual sustenance for God-realization. This is the process which results in a purified personality. There is nothing abstract about tazkiyah. It is a known reality. Tazkiyah is the result of a struggle on the part of the individual. It is not at all related to any mysterious inspiration from some supposedly saintly person.

The Incentive to Purify Oneself

A tradition recorded in the books of Hadith is set forth here in the words of Musnad Ahmad:

> *"On the Day of Judgement, when all the people of Paradise have entered Paradise and all the people of Hell have entered Hell, Death will be brought there in the form of a white sheep. It will be made to stand between Heaven and Hell. Then it will be said, 'O People of Paradise, do you recognize it?' They will look up to it and say, 'Yes, it is Death.' After this the people of Hell will be asked, 'O People of Hell, do you recognize this?' They will look up and say, 'Yes, it is Death.' After this the order will be given for Death to be slaughtered. Then, it will be said, 'O People of Paradise, now you have eternity and no*

death, and O People of Hell, now you have eternity and no death.'" (Musnad Ahmad, Hadith No. 11066)

What is purification? Purification means making oneself a purified soul, such as will be worthy of inhabiting the refined environment of Paradise. On Doomsday, the purified individuals will be ushered into Paradise and the unpurified individuals will be cast into Hell. After this it will be announced that the law of death has been ended. Now both parties have to abide eternally in their places. This will be a unique moment. The people of Paradise will be in a state of bliss for having found the eternal world of happiness. On the contrary, the people of Hell will experience indescribable remorse—an eternal torment over what has become their lot because of not having purified their souls. This perception is undoubtedly a powerful incentive to undertaking the process of purification.

Paradise for the Purified Soul

According to Chapter 20 of the Quran, Paradise is for one who purifies his soul in this present world and reaches the world Hereafter with a purified personality. This reality has been clearly described in many verses of the Quran. Attainment of Paradise will be based on individual merit rather than on personal affiliation to any community or group.

Paradise, therefore, is only for the individual who purifies himself. Purification means abandoning a life of unawareness and leading a life ruled by the conscience. A person has to save himself from anything which comes in the path of truth, and when he faces any hurdles, he must not resort to expediency. When desires arise within him, he must crush them, and when he is overtaken by arrogance, he should be able to overcome his overweening pride.

Tazkiyah means purifying the individual of unfavourable elements, so that he may reach the point of perfection in a favourable environment. This was a very important task given to the prophets.

A prophet makes the greatest possible efforts to prepare human beings whose hearts are free from the love of all else except the love of God. He strives to bring into existence such souls as are free from complexes and are worthy of receiving the divine provision from the universe.

Purification is the principal condition for entry into Paradise. Without purification, one can never gain entry into the eternal heavenly abode.

Hadith—A Source of Tazkiyah

A scholar once said: "Any person who has a collection of Hadith in his house, is as if in the presence of the Prophet who is in conversation with him."

The above-mentioned saying is not only about what the Prophet had to say, but by implication, it also indicates a form of companionship with the Prophet.

None of the sayings of the Prophet of Islam recorded in the Books of Hadith are purely abstract in sense. Indeed, every saying has a special background. That is to say, the Prophet on different occasions faced a variety of situations and, in accordance with the demands of each situation, he gave people advice. In this way, each saying of the Prophet of Islam relates to particular sets of circumstances. All the sayings of the Prophet are of topical relevance.

If the individual deepens his understanding of the Hadith and conceptualizes the background to it, this in itself will be like being in the presence of the Prophet. He will perceive that he is not only reading the sayings of the Prophet in a book, but is also reading between the lines of the Prophet's sayings and thus mentally refreshing himself about their background. If the reader of the Hadith is enthusiastic about it, he will feel as if he is actually experiencing the companionship of the Prophet. In this way, there will be a manifold enhancement of his understanding of the Hadith.

On reflection, it will be realized that the reader of the Hadith is not just a reader: he is more of a "listener" seated along with the Companions in the presence of the Prophet of Islam. This is one of the creative ways of studying the Hadith. And studying the traditions of the Prophet in this creative manner is undoubtedly the greatest source of purification.

Tazkiyah–A Continuous Process

Aisha, the wife of the Prophet of Islam, says of him:

> *"On every occasion, the Prophet of Islam remembered God." (Sahih Muslim, Hadith no. 373).*

This tradition shows the prophetic way of purification, that is to say that the Prophet purified himself on all occasions. This shows that tazkiyah is not the name of any short training course, but is rather a continuous process. When a believer discovers the truth, due to the awakening of his conscience, every event or experience in his life becomes a point of reference for his purification. This enables him to receive spiritual nourishment on a daily basis. In this way, this process of tazkiyah continues till his last breath. Just as physical energy is generated by constant nourishment, so also is tazkiyah achieved by constant effort.

There is the general impression, however, that a brief training course is all that it takes to attain a state of tazkiyah. That is, it is just like receiving religious education in a seminary within the limited frame of a short-term prescribed course of study. But the truth is that this is an underestimation of tazkiyah.

Tazkiyah, a cumulative process, and not the result of any fixed practice, requires an awakened mind. It is attained through an unflagging intellectual process and not by engaging in any temporary course of study.

The Process of De-Conditioning

Tazkiyah, a continuous process, goes on day in and day out. When it does not happen in this way, there is a hadith which describes the result of this:

> *"The heart becomes covered with rust, just like iron when*

it comes in contact with water." A question was asked: "O Prophet! What is the way to purify or clean one's heart?" The Prophet replied, "Remembering death often and studying the Quran." (Shu'ab al-Iman, al-Bayhaqi, Hadith no. 1859).

This tradition of the Prophet tells us of a psychological reality. That is, in the context of the society he lives in, a person has repeatedly to undergo such experiences as produce negative feelings within him, for instance, anger, hatred, violence, revenge, and so on. An individual ought to bury these feelings instantly, for, if he fails to do so, they will become a permanent presence in the human mind, and a time will come when it will be almost impossible to eliminate them.

There are two major parts of the human mind, the conscious and the unconscious. It is quite natural for negative feelings to first of all enter the conscious part of the mind. If such feelings are not immediately cast out from the mind, they gradually reach the unconscious part of the mind, from where it becomes difficult to eradicate them. One should always remain vigilant about this. At all times a person should keep converting his negativity into positivity. That is, he must de-condition his conditioned mind in order to purify it and keep it free from pollution. The only way of purification, or de-conditioning, is to repeatedly remind himself of death and to reflect on the purpose of life.

Tazkiyah–Spiritual Nourishment

The body requires physical food. When it receives its food, it becomes healthy. Similarly, the soul requires spiritual provision. When the soul is provided with such food, it becomes healthy. This process is called purification of the soul and this healthy soul is called a purified and cleansed soul.

According to the Quran, the food for the soul is in thinking (3:191). At every moment certain incidents take place in the life of a person. These incidents appear at the level of society, history, the universe, and so on.

Thinking about these incidents or events and deriving lessons from them, is food for the soul.

One who develops his consciousness to such an extent that he sees the glory of God in the events which take place around him, and for whom these events become a means of remembering God, has obtained the divine provision for his soul. His soul will continue to receive this healthy nourishment until he finally leaves this world to be ushered into the Divine Presence.

The most important source of tazkiyah is the lessons one learns to take from every happening. The ability to learn lessons is the basis of tazkiyah. This is the soil from which tazkiyah grows. Trying to encourage its growth at any other place is like trying to grow a green tree on a rock. The source of tazkiyah is divine provision and not human provision. It is the result of that process which is directly established between God and man through a psychological relationship. Tazkiyah is not achieved through any intermediary between God and man. Tazkiyah is a blessing which one directly receives from God.

Ijtihad is not Permissible in Worship

A religious scholar once visited a well-known Sufi hospice, where he found that people were engaged in loud recitation (zikr bil jahr) and other such rituals. On observing this, the scholar cited a tradition of the Prophet according to which

> *"anyone who invents anything in this religion which is not part of it stands rejected." (Sahih al-Bukhari, Hadith no. 2697).*

The scholar said that these Sufi rituals were not prevalent at the time of the Prophet and his Companions, therefore, they would be regarded as innovations. The Sufi replied that what is forbidden in the Hadith is innovation in religion (ihdath fil-amr). It does not forbid innovation for religion (ihdath lil-amr), and all the practices of tasawwuf are of the nature of innovation for religion.

This explanation of this tradition is unacademic. If we consider its exact wording, it has no basis in the Hadith. That is, something that has been added to the religion the Prophet has bequeathed to his people is expressed as 'what is not in it.' In such a case, the problem is not that of a change of preposition; the real problem is whether or not the religion that we received from the Prophet of Islam contained what now presents itself as an addition of later times. It is an established fact that rituals such as repeated loud recitations of Quranic phrases were not practiced in the religion handed down to us by the Prophet. Religious scholars are agreed on their stand that there can be no guesswork in religious worship. That is, no ijtihad will be engaged in in the matter of worship, in which domain any inference or argument will be held valid only when it is based on the religious texts, the Quran and the Hadith. Exercising ijtihad based on anything else is, from the religious point of view, both unscholarly and unacceptable.

Tazkiyah at Every Moment

There is the general misconception that tazkiyah is a temporary course of action or that, to achieve it, some particular words or phrases have to be recited at fixed times. But this ritualistic form of tazkiyah is unnatural: nothing can be achieved by resorting to such short-term methods.

The truth is that, just as one inhales oxygen at every moment—there being no temporary way of inhaling—tazkiyah too is a continuous process. The real tazkiyah is that which continues at every moment. For instance, in this couplet by a Persian poet:

> *Bar mazar-e-ma ghariban, nay charaghe, nay guley,*
> *Nay par-e-parvana raqsad, Nay sadai bulbule*
>
> *(I being a poor man, there is no lamp, no flower on my*

grave, no fly hovers around my grave, no nightingale chirps at my grave).

When a couplet like this comes to mind, you should first think how deep a state of ignorance the poet is in. He is thinking of the lamp and the flower at his grave. But the real problem is that, after death, one reaches another world, the demands of which are different from those of the present world. In that world certain superior qualities will be required, over and above those possessed in this world. Furthermore, there will be no time for preparation in the next world. There we shall find only the result of today's actions: there will be no opportunities to take remedial action.

The result of such revised thinking will be that this couplet, which people recite purely for enjoyment, will teach the individual a great lesson. He will start preparing himself for developing such a personality as will bring him success in the world of the Hereafter. With this mental re-orientation, he will start thinking about what he will undergo after death, instead of what the fate of his grave will be.

Introspection after Making a Mistake

Introspection is a major source of tazkiyah. Introspection awakens the human mind, it jolts the human personality, it gives the individual the incentive to reform himself. In this way introspection leads one to intellectual and spiritual development.

For instance, suppose someone said something which hurt you, you were provoked and you reacted negatively. Later, you became repentant and engaged in introspection, which led you to think that by having behaved in this way, you were developing a negative personality, such as would have a deleterious effect in the life after death. Such a negative personality would, indeed, render one incapable of gaining entry into Paradise.

You came to realize that the culture of the people of Paradise would be that of peace; only those would be accommodated there who had the capacity to live together in love and peace. This being so, one who develops a personality which is intolerant, easily provoked and downright unfriendly will be held ineligible to enter Paradise and will be deprived of happiness and success for all eternity. Such thinking will prove to be revolutionary and you will become your own watchdog. You will become extremely keen to reform yourself. Thinking born of introspection is the greatest source of tazkiyah. Tazkiyah can always be achieved by inner self-appraisal, rather than by some external activity.

Heart-based Tazkiyah, Mind-based Tazkiyah

Study the last part of the third chapter of the Quran which exhorts people of understanding to reflect on the signs in the creation of the heavens and the earth so that they should realize their Lord. Through these signs, you will learn of the Creation Plan of God, you will discover Heaven and Hell, and you will comprehend the importance of the Prophet, in short, all those things which are related directly or indirectly to tazkiyah. In all these verses of the Quran the realization of God is linked with pondering over the universe. In other words, tazkiyah, according to the Quran, is based on the mind and not on the heart. In this connection the word 'heart' is used in the Quran and the Hadith in the literary sense and not in the physical sense. In later times, Muslims came under the influence of the Sufis, who believed in the concept of tazkiyah based on the heart.

According to this concept, it came to be accepted that the human heart was the treasure house of all divine realities. It was believed that one could reach this treasure house through meditation and then one would attain tazkiyah. But this concept of heart-based tazkiyah was not derived from the Quran. It was in fact derived from history. This concept of heart-based spirituality had its origin in ancient times and, as a matter of tradition, people introduced it into Islam.

Modern science has provided the scientific foundation by which Islamic tazkiyah, based on the mind, can once again be revived. Modern research has proved that the human heart functions only as a pump for the circulation of the blood. The heart has no capacity to think. The mind alone possesses the capacity to think. All human actions come into existence through thinking and the way to attain tazkiyah is no exception. Tazkiyah is achieved at the level of the mind, rather than through any strivings at the level of the heart. For the attainment of tazkiyah, paying attention to the heart is as infructuous as paying attention to one's nails or hair or anything else.

The Need of a Guide

In principle, the path to tazkiyah for a person is to reflect upon the Quran and to study the Hadith in order to find guidance from the lives of the Prophet and the Companions of the Prophet. This is the basic source of tazkiyah, and its importance will last for all eternity. Besides this, there is also a practical way of attaining tazkiyah, and that is to find a living guide, thus benefitting from his learning and experience. When a guide is found, he ought to be accepted as such unconditionally. Making conditions before accepting a guide only sets up a hurdle in the path of tazkiyah.

When anyone says that he has accepted someone unconditionally, this does not mean that he has entered into this arrangement with blind faith. It only means that, as a result of the development of moral consciousness, two human beings have come together on the same wavelength. This is a case of intellectual affinity, rather than a case of blind faith. When two human beings reach the core of truth, they naturally enter a state of intellectual commonality. They become, as it were, intellectual "twins".

A guide is essential for the attainment of tazkiyah, but the importance of the guide is practical rather than a matter of creed. The importance of a guide, in actual fact, relates directly to the general way (sunnah) of God. This way has been described in the following verse of the Quran: "It is We who distribute among them their livelihood in the life of this world, and raise some of them above others in rank, so that they may take one another into service." (43:32). This verse shows that it is not the way of God to bestow on everyone the qualities required for a guide. It is the way of God to give leadership qualities to particular persons and others are required to follow them. This is the natural system of life according to the way of God.

The case of a religious guide also relates directly to this way of God, for God grants special help to those who have to perform this role. The duty of tazkiyah-seekers is to recognize them, and receive guidance from them in order to achieve their objective. Those who fail to do so will be treated as failures in this test of nature.

There is nothing mysterious about this. It falls within a known and natural sphere and can be understood upon reflection. What is received from a religious guide is not something mysterious in nature: it is the same as what in general terms is called a training course. A religious guide is a living guide rather than a sacred personality in some mysterious sense of the word.

The Importance of Interaction for Tazkiyah

Companionship is a very helpful means of attaining tazkiyah. In ancient times, face-to-face meeting was the sole way of having companionship.

In the present age, people may be living at great distances from each other, so that companionship may appear to be out of the question. Yet it is still possible for the tazkiyah-seeker to have the benefits of his guide's companionship through tele-counselling, which is more immediate than communicating by means of letters or books, as was formerly done. If anyone is a seeker of tazkiyah in the real sense, the new channels of communication will serve as a viable alternative to actual companionship.

The printing press, one of these modern means of communication, has made it possible to learn about tazkiyah on a continuous basis through reading material such as books and magazines. These have to be seriously studied if the tazkiyah-seeker is to become really familiar with the subject. From the Quran itself (96:4), we come to know of the importance of this method of learning from the written word, that is, imbibing the spirit of religion through books.

In one respect, the importance of study is not less than that of companionship. Indeed, the consistent study of books enables one to think deeply on the subject. Yet, although the study of books is of great benefit, interaction is still essential for tazkiyah, because that facilitates a fruitful exchange of ideas. That is, one must keep in touch with the religious guide and seek guidance from him in all matters. This contact can be made through direct meetings or through other means of communication. Such contact is necessary on a daily basis; occasional contact will not serve the purpose.

Without Mediation

Consciously or unconsciously, people generally think that tazkiyah requires some mysterious mediation, say, of past saintly figures or great men of learning, or some religious guide who has attained a high degree of spirituality. According to this mysterious concept of mediation, the religious guide (shaikh) himself becomes the goal, or the focus, whereas it is God Who must be at the centre, and the position of the religious guide must be purely peripheral, i.e., as a means to an end.

The concept of mediation is entirely without foundation. Tazkiyah is attained through contact with God, without any mediation; no mediation can be of any help in this matter.

Tazkiyah in reality is bestowed by God. There is no need of mediation to receive this gift from God. God directly bestows whatever He wills on all human beings; the condition for this to happen is to become a seeker of tazkiyah in real earnest.

The Quran says:

> *"When My servants ask you about Me, say that I am near. I respond to the call of one who calls, whenever he*

*calls to Me: let them, then, respond to Me, and believe in
Me, so that they may be rightly guided." (Quran 2:186)*

The word "near" used in the above verse of the Quran shows that the means of attaining tazkiyah is to come close to God rather than rely upon mediation or a mediator. He, who wants to purify himself, ought to awaken his mind and make efforts to come as near to God as possible.

No mediation can ever be helpful in achieving this goal. Tazkiyah can only be attained directly from God. There is no other way of attaining tazkiyah. The truth is that the concept of mediation is an obstacle in the path of tazkiyah. When God is closer to man than "his jugular vein" (Quran 50:16), why should there be any need for mediation?

The concept of mediation stems from the notion that there can be a mysterious relationship between a human being and God, whereas the concept of a religious guide is established at a conscious level between the follower and the guide.

Prior to Tazkiyah

The real incentive to the attainment of tazkiyah is the feeling of being devoid of spiritual resources. The more one acknowledges one's feeling of need, the more one feels the necessity for tazkiyah. One so motivated will naturally seek fulfilment of this need.

This discovery starts with one's own existence. First of all, man consciously discovers his own existence. This discovery arouses his curiosity as to who is his Creator. In this way he discovers his Creator. This discovery produces a tremendous feeling of the greatness of his Creator.

Then he reflects that, as a needy person in the fullest sense of the word, he has been unable to fulfil any of his needs by dint of his own strength. It is not by his own efforts that all the basic things he requires are already there for him—earth, water, air oxygen, light, food and all those numerous things which are known to be constituents of the life support system. All are there for him as unconditional gifts. After this discovery, he attempts to understand who is the giver of all these blessings. In this way, he discovers his Lord. As a result of this, an immense amount of love is engendered within him for the Giver.

His search then leads him to the question: what is his goal? Then he learns that he cannot reach his desired goal in the present world. This discovery finally makes him extremely desirous of Paradise, where he may attain his goal and have a life of fulfilment.

In a similar way, when he goes further in this thinking, he discovers that he needs authentic guidance for his life. Then he comes to the conclusion that, despite every effort, he cannot find such guidance on his own. This discovery leads him to the reality that the only possible source of authentic guidance is a prophet. He thus wholeheartedly accepts the Prophet as his guide. After all these discoveries, he naturally becomes a modest person. He begins to live in the greatness of God. God's creations become a perpetual impetus to His remembrance. He accepts the Prophet as the perfect guide and Paradise becomes his greatest goal. These are the experiences relating to the realization of God which can be described as tazkiyah.

Tazkiyah and Introspection

Tazkiyah is not a one-time course. That is, it is not possible to take a course for a temporary period and become a permanently purified person. The truth is that purification is a continuous process, which lasts for a lifetime. Tazkiyah is an act of introspection, in which one has to monitor one's own actions. One who is desirous of tazkiyah must be careful about his speech and actions at every moment. With total objectivity, he must repeatedly engage in self-appraisal. This process of introspection is set in only in one who repents and does introspection.

This present world—a testing ground—has been created by the Creator in such a way that at every moment one is beset by trials. Repeatedly faced with the demands of the self, satanic temptations may lead him to do something undesirable; and unfavourable circumstances, coupled with a bad environment, may cause one to fall a prey to evil influences. All such failings run counter to tazkiyah.

A person should be so sensitive in this matter that, on each such occasion of temptation, he immediately becomes alert to the immanent dangers and then does one's utmost to re-purify oneself. Re-purifying oneself on such occasions is tazkiyah. But without introspection, no one can become a purified personality. Introspection leads to intellectual development, which is a guarantee that the process of tazkiyah will continue to take place.

Tazkiyah and Modesty

No crops can grow on barren land. Requiring favourable soil for their growth, they must grow on fertile land. So also does tazkiyah require favourable soil from which to grow. And that favourable soil is modesty. The quality of modesty greatly facilitates the attainment of tazkiyah. On the contrary, arrogance is unfavourable to its attainment. An arrogant person can never attain the goal of self-purification. The most significant feature of modesty is that it causes a person to feel that there is something lacking in him.

The result of this feeling is that when the truth becomes evident to him, he accepts it without any reservation. He receives it in an unbiased way and soon discovers that this truth can compensate for his shortcomings. Thus, he accepts the truth as if it belonged to him. This quality is the spirit, or essence, of tazkiyah. The case of an arrogant person is quite the opposite. The thinking of an arrogant person is that he already has everything and need not take anything from anyone. For this reason, he is not able to accept advice from others. He rejects the message of the reformer. This attitude becomes an obstacle to his taking to the path of tazkiyah.

The truth is that tazkiyah, a continuous process, can have its effect only on a modest person. Modesty enables one to accept the truth and frees one from psychological complexes. Only a complex-free soul (Quran 89:27) can succeed in attaining the goal of tazkiyah.

Prophetic Prayers

Many traditions have been recorded in the books of Hadith, which tell us that the Prophet used to recite certain words of prayer at certain times. These words are generally known as masnoon dhikr, or masnoon dua. Generally, it is believed that these words recited by the Prophet are the greatest source of tazkiyah, and that one should learn them and keep reciting them on certain occasions in order to achieve the ends of tazkiyah.

However, this is not true. These words uttered by the Prophet are in actual fact a reflection of the feelings or the states of mind of the Prophet. The truth is that the Prophet of Islam, because of his high level of realization, used to be preoccupied by thoughts of God. On different occasions this inner feeling found expression in words. Today, those who study books of Hadith only know the words of the Prophet: they stop short of knowing his feelings or states of mind. This is why they take the words to be all in all. Subscribing to this concept of prophetic prayers is to underestimate the words of the Prophet.

In its reality, prophetic prayer is meant to awaken one's consciousness. Then it is only through the continual thinking process thus initiated that we may develop such a personality as lives in thoughts of God. This is, as it were, the first prerequisite for learning from the prayers of the Prophet. After this the words of prayer uttered by him will be of great importance so far as the development of a spiritual personality is concerned. Without this preparation, repeating the words of the Prophet, rather than following the words of the Prophet in the real sense, is nothing but empty repetition.

People, consciously or unconsciously, regard the prayers of the Prophet as having been couched in sacred words, which possess mysterious qualities. But this is not true. The truth is that the prayers of the Prophet tell us of the states of mind of the Prophet, rather than being just words in the simple sense.

Tazkiyah and Prayer

What is prayer (dua)? Prayer is an expression in words of the feeling which is produced after a helpless person discovers Almighty God. The prayers of the Prophet are also an expression of these feelings for Almighty God. They are not just another name for a set of words uttered by the Prophet on certain occasions. The Prophet's prayers are, in actual fact, spiritual discoveries, far from a mere utterance of a set of words.

According to a Hadith Qudsi (Hadith Qudsi is the hadith in which the Prophet says that God says so and so), the Prophet observed:

> *"I am with the expectations of My servant, so he ought to have good expectations about Me." (Dakhirah al-Huffaz, Ibn al-Qaisarani, Hadith No. 6541)*

What is this hope or expectation? It relates in actual fact to one's discovering certain attribute of God, and then on the basis of this discovery, having good expectations of God: that is, seeking goodness from God.

For instance, the Quran says:

> *"He has given you all that you asked of Him." (Quran 14:34).*

This verse provides a point of reference to man who may invoke God's blessings thus:

> *"O God, I was not even aware of my needs in the life of this world that I should have asked You for those things. You on Your own arranged for all my requirements to be met in my worldly life. Now, in the life Hereafter, I ask You to provide me with all the things I require in the next world."*

This kind of prayer always comes to one's lips after a great psychological turmoil. Another name for this psychological storm is tazkiyah. Tazkiyah and prayer are interdependent. Tazkiyah will always be followed by dua.

Praying to God is a proof that the process of tazkiyah is at work. There is no tazkiyah without prayer, and vice versa.

The Form of Tazkiyah

There is no visible form of tazkiyah. Had there been a fixed form of tazkiyah, a person would think, consciously or unconsciously that, by observing that form, he had completed the course of tazkiyah. In this way, he would become content. But the feeling of contentment in this matter is very harmful. It is essential for the attainment of tazkiyah that one should always have a certain feeling of inadequacy. Such a feeling makes one continuously strive to undergo the process of tazkiyah, whereas any feeling of contentment blocks the incentive to make unremitting efforts.

Tazkiyah and the Islamic way of worship are closely interrelated. Neither can be separated from the other. No one can say that he has completed the process of tazkiyah and is therefore no longer required to perform the acts of worship ordained in Islam.

But this does not mean that the performance of the form of worship in itself is sufficient to serve the purpose of tazkiyah. The correct position is that worship is an external manifestation of the spirit of tazkiyah. If the spirit of tazkiyah is produced within one, in the real sense, then inevitably one will become God's worshipper. Worship cannot be separated from tazkiyah.

But full emphasis should be laid upon producing the spirit of tazkiyah, rather than upon the external form of worship. It would be true to say that, without worship, the claim to have attained tazkiyah is false. But it is also a fact that the outward form of worship cannot automatically produce the spirit of tazkiyah.

Conscience—A Guide to Tazkiyah

Man is endowed with a natural faculty called the conscience, which serves as a divine teacher and a guide to tazkiyah. Conscience guides one on all occasions, albeit wordlessly—do this, don't do that, this behaviour is in accordance with tazkiyah and that behaviour is against tazkiyah, this behaviour will help in developing a purified personality and that behaviour will defile your personality.

But experience shows that the majority of the people do not allow their conscience to act as a guide to tazkiyah. What is the reason for this? The reason is that everyone is given another faculty, which is the opposite of conscience, and that is the ego. A person often comes under the influence of the self, or Satan. He does not let the conscience work for him. The voice of the conscience can be heard on all occasions, but the ego suppresses that voice and renders it ineffective.

It is essential for a seeker of tazkiyah to be abreast of this reality, so that he awakens his power of thinking, and nullifies his ego on all occasions. The moment one is able to overcome one's ego, one's conscience will be able to play its natural role and one will be able to traverse the path of tazkiyah without any deviation. The exercise of nullifying the ego or reducing it to zero has a decisive role to play. But no one can perform this task for another. One has to do it oneself; the moment one's ego is awakened, one should become alert and by exercising one's will power set one's ego at naught.

The Method of Tazkiyah

Many attempts have been made to describe a number of methods of tazkiyah. Lists of these methods have also been prepared. But the truth is that there is no list that can be prepared for the method of tazkiyah. This is because no list, however long it may be, can be complete. No list can cover all the methods of tazkiyah, and later experiences will prove that that "long" list was also less than complete.

The truth is that tazkiyah relates not to some list but is the product rather of one's own will and intention. If a person were indeed serious about tazkiyah and wanted to attain it honestly, he would certainly succeed in this. But if he is not totally serious about it and shows no eagerness about attaining it, then no amount of writing or speeches will suffice for his self-purification.

It is a unique quality of a human being that he is able to find justification for every mistake he makes. He is always able to find beautiful words to portray his faults as virtues and his mistakes as right action. This being so, no reformer or well-wisher can bring about the tazkiyah of this kind of person. To attain tazkiyah, one must take a conscious decision about oneself. This decision should be so firm that one remains steadfastly true to it and makes no excuses to renege upon it.

What is required for tazkiyah is will power. This should be so firm that it remains unaffected by any temptation or any fear of damage to worldly interests. The will must be resistant to any form of pressure. One who aims at self purification should be willing to do whatever religion requires him to do, whatever the cost at the practical and psychological levels.

The Need for Intellectual Awareness

One method of attaining tazkiyah is to formulate certain principles in an abstract way, put them in writing and ask others to read them. This may be one way to achieve tazkiyah, but the more effective way is to relate those principles to some situation. One form of this second method requires a living spiritual guide. Another method is for one to develop his thinking to the point of discovering on his own the element of tazkiyah in every experience or observation, and then making that experience or observation a part of his thinking.

Abū Dharr, a Companion of the Prophet, once said that even if the Prophet saw a bird flying in the air with outstretched wings, he would give them some lesson in the realization of God. (Musnad Aḥmad, Hadith No. 21361). This is an example of imparting education in tazkiyah with reference to some situation.

The fact is that there is no abstract method of effectively achieving tazkiyah. The only way is for a person to make himself so intellectually aware that he can develop in himself the ability "to learn a lesson" (15:75). He may relate the situation confronting him to tazkiyah and then learn a spiritual lesson from it. In everyday experiences, we have the stuff of tazkiyah. Learn to see daily experiences from this standpoint, then every experience and every observation will become for you a stepping stone to tazkiyah.

Activating One's Thinking

Traditionally, some things are considered to be the means of attaining tazkiyah, such as, supererogatory prayers, recitation of the Qur'an, prophetic prayers, meditation, companionship, taking lessons from the lives of the "saints", and so on. According to this thinking, tazkiyah is like a fixed course, or something to be learned from a manual. However, the truth is that there is no fixed course for attaining tazkiyah. Tazkiyah can be attained only through a living act. The real means of attaining the ends of tazkiyah is for a person to reflect on the signs of God, activate his thinking, and through continuous reflection or pondering, discover the deeper realities of things. This discovery is spiritual food for a person who is a seeker of tazkiyah.

For instance, suppose you see a bird. This reminds you of this saying of the Prophet that the hearts of the people of Paradise will be like the hearts of birds. (Ṣaḥīḥ Muslim, Hadith No. 2840). You later begin to think about yourself—whether or not your heart is like that of the bird; whether or not your heart is free of all negative thinking like that of the bird; whether or not you are free from greed like the bird; whether or not you are as harmless as a bird; whether or not you follow the law of nature, just as the bird does. Such thinking is the essence of tazkiyah. Without such introspection, no one can attain tazkiyah.

In its reality, tazkiyah is an act of spiritually developing one's own self. In engaging in self-purification, one has to become one's own teacher and has to purify oneself. Sitting in the company of another or listening to someone else's preaching cannot in itself be effective for one who aspires to tazkiyah. Initial guidance can be provided by another person, but taking it to completion is a task one must achieve oneself. In the process of attaining tazkiyah, if the share of the other person is 1% then one's own share is 99%.

Tazkiyah—A Source of Intellectual Development

Tazkiyah literally means purification. In the extended sense it means growth. In this respect, tazkiyah means intellectual development.

The mind is not something stagnant, it is ever-growing, like a tree. It is this process which is called "adding faith to their faith" (48:4) in the Qur'an. Adding faith to faith means development in consciousness, which is another name for intellectual development. The real faith is one which does not stagnate, but grows continuously in its conviction about God.

How does tazkiyah or intellectual development take place? The path to this is contemplation. Contemplation is in itself a continuous process—contemplating on the Qur'an and ḥadith, the life of the Prophet, the lives of the Companions, the various human disciplines, the universe, the earth and the heavens. There is also the kind of contemplation which takes place during serious discussions. In this process of contemplation, new ideas emerge, deeper meanings come to light, new aspects hitherto unexplored of different events and realities are discovered.

For one who possesses true faith, every study and observation will become a means of divine discovery; every experience will bring him closer to God. If initially, his faith is in the form of a seed, it will keep growing and assume the form of a fully-grown tree—tazkiyah is the Islamic name for this intellectual and spiritual process. Faith initially brings us into the fold of Islam, then tazkiyah helps in the development of this faith.

Tazkiyah and Knowledge

According to one point of view regarding the method of tazkiyah, the company of a Ṣūfī who has attained the state of realization is a must, because just one glance from such a person is considered enough to bring about a change in the human psyche. But this point of view cannot be substantiated by either the Qurʾan or the ḥadith. According to the Qurʾan and the ḥadith, tazkiyah can be attained only by one's own reflection and introspection. If one has developed right thinking, by studying the relevant books and by observation of nature, one will derive lessons which will help one in purifying one's personality.

Chapter 35 of the Qurʾan mentions mountains in which there are streaks of various shades. Then the verse goes on to say,

> *"Only those of His servants, who possess knowledge, fear God." (35:28).*

This verse shows that the knowledge of mountains or natural events should create awe and fear of God in a person. That is to say, the source of fear is learning. The more learning one acquires, the more one will be able to understand the wisdom in God's creation.

Study increases the capacity to think. Study enables one to derive the food of God-realization from things at a deeper level. For instance, everyone inhales the air for the oxygen it provides. It is thus possible for everyone to be thankful to God for this. However, a person who has any knowledge of modern discoveries about the respiratory system, will be a thousand times more grateful, and thus his tazkiyah will also develop to a much greater degree than one who does not know of these discoveries.

The fact is that knowledge provides a wide framework for developing one's tazkiyah. Through knowledge, which is like a booster, one discovers new aspects of increasing tazkiyah.

Save Yourself from Distraction

One principle of success in this world is to abandon one thing in favour of another. It is human psychology that one cannot focus on two things at a time. If a person focuses on one thing, his mind will be diverted from another. This same principle applies to tazkiyah. Also, one who wants to engage in self-purification will necessarily have to totally abandon all things irrelevant to tazkiyah.

The greatest obstacle in the path of tazkiyah is distraction. It is essential for the seeker of tazkiyah to make tazkiyah his supreme goal; to keep himself totally away from all things related to distraction. Concentration is essential for tazkiyah, one who does not have the capacity to concentrate will certainly fall far short of the attainment of tazkiyah.

Everything has its price and tazkiyah too has its price. That price is keeping oneself away from all kinds of distraction, for instance, family entertainment programmes, friendship culture, the love of food, clothes, the craving for fame and wealth and other temptations in life. All such things for a seeker of tazkiyah amount to distraction. Anyone who wants to purify himself must distance himself totally from all such things.

Tazkiyah gives one a noble character and enables one to be deserving of angels' company. Tazkiyah brings one closer to God. Without this a person is like dry wood; whereas with tazkiyah, one becomes a green tree. Tazkiyah is not something mysterious: it can be equated with an awakening of the consciousness of faith.

Tazkiyah and the Demands of the Times

The mindset of the people differs from age to age. One accepts something only when it is in accordance with one's way of thinking. This is what is called the addressing of the mind. Just as making concessions to the human mind is necessary in other matters, it is likewise necessary in the matter of tazkiyah as well.

In ancient times the way of thinking was traditional but the modern age is that of scientific thinking. To bring about tazkiyah in people of the present times, it is essential to speak to them in a way that addresses their minds. The source of tazkiyah in present times is exactly the same as it was in ancient times. However, there is a difference of approach between the two—that of manner of speech and reasoning. In ancient times the traditional ways were effective for people of that age, but, in present times, for effective tazkiyah, it is essential to change the style of speech. Only then will it be possible for the modern man to understand the importance of tazkiyah and adopt it in his life.

For instance, in ancient times, the word 'purification' or 'reform' of the self was used. This word could address the ancient traditional mind. However, the modern man can understand this subject better if we change our wording or mode of addressing the subject. That is, we have to consider that every person, for various reasons, is a case for the conditioning of the mind. For the purpose of a human being's reform, it is essential to de-condition his mind, i.e., re-engineer his mind to make him capable of seeing reality 'as it is' and thus form accurate opinions. To address people's minds, according to this style of tazkiyah, it is essential for the guide or teacher, to possess a vast knowledge of both ancient and modern learning, without which the task of tazkiyah cannot be effectively performed with the modern man.

The Condition of Tazkiyah

Tazkiyah is not just some technical science. Technical science can be expressed fully in words, whereas tazkiyah is a science of realization and, as such can be only partially expressed in words. Every facet of tazkiyah requires some addition which can only be produced by the seeker of tazkiyah.

It is necessary for the attainment of tazkiyah that the seeker of tazkiyah be totally serious in his quest. This means that his mind should be prepared, that he should be very keen to learn, be free of all kinds of prejudices, be a complex-free soul, have the ability to see things as they are, be capable of rising above personal predilections, and have the ability to stand up to criticism, or should welcome criticism just as he welcomes praise; he should be ready to accept the truth without any preconditions and readily concede his mistakes. Finally, he must see things from the right angle.

Two parties are involved in the process of tazkiyah—the teacher and the seeker. The role of neither is 100%: both have to perform 50% of the task. The role of the teacher is that of a guide in the real sense. He should have understood the subject so thoroughly by a deeper study of the Qur'an and the ḥadīth that he is able to explain it in the best possible way.

In this matter the other half role is to be played by the seeker. The seeker must be fully capable of acceptance; he must come out of his conditioning to understand the message; he must be able to rise above his fixed mindset and be able to give importance to the truth and not to 'who said it'. One who has all these qualities can successfully follow the path of tazkiyah.

The Acceptance of Reality

By the highest standard of humanity, one should be able to accept the reality or truth. This is very important for every human being. And the discovery of reality must result in its acknowledgement. If someone is unaware of the reality, he will be reckoned an ignorant person. If after the discovery of reality, a person fails to express it publicly, this amounts to living by double standards or being hypocritical.

This is no simple act. It is, in fact, a development of the human personality along the right lines, and tazkiyah is only the other name for this development of the human personality.

There is nothing mysterious about tazkiyah. Tazkiyah is the result of the awakening of such consciousness as enables a person to attribute everything to God; every experience becomes a means of bringing him closer to God. It is through these experiences that a personality develops which may be called a purified personality.

The truth is that the whole matter is one of right or wrong attribution. Wrongly attributing events to anyone other than God is to pollute one's soul. This is to deprive oneself of the opportunity to purify oneself. On the contrary, when one attributes events to the true Creator, one emancipates and uplifts one's soul. By availing of all such opportunities, one develops one's personality by purifying one's soul. Tazkiyah cannot be attained in a vacuum; it comes about in the course of the everyday events of life. What is required for tazkiyah is an awakened mind, rather than some mysterious action performed in seclusion.

Tazkiyah and Sacrifice

The attainment of tazkiyah is no simple matter: it always requires some sacrifice, which is psychological rather than physical in nature. This sacrifice is to completely renounce, for the sake of tazkiyah, those things that run counter to acquiring tazkiyah. It is a principle of nature that in order to achieve something, one has to let go of some other thing. This principle is as important in the case of tazkiyah as in any other case.

One of the things to rid oneself of is bad habits. Due to environmental influences, every man and woman becomes accustomed to certain habits which are detrimental to the attainment of tazkiyah. It is absolutely necessary for a seeker of tazkiyah to totally rid himself of such habits. Some of these habits include speaking excessively without thinking, busying oneself with the demands of one's family, taking a lot of interest in eating and clothes, pursuing the culture of entertainment, speaking to others of someone's negative points or shortcomings, going shopping and on outings, spending extravagantly instead of limiting oneself to one's needs, having superficial tastes, becoming angry at criticism and feeling happy when praised, being greedy for material things, not restricting oneself to one's needs and preferring affectations to simplicity.

Everything has a price and there is a price for attaining tazkiyah, that is, abstaining from everything that goes against achieving this goal. A person who wants to attain tazkiyah, but is not ready to give up all that which prevents one from attaining tazkiyah, is certainly not serious in his quest. Tazkiyah can never become a reality if the seeker is of a non-serious temperament. A frivolous mentality and tazkiyah do not go together.

A person who is serious in his pursuit of tazkiyah will himself realize which things are favourable to tazkiyah and which are not. His sincerity will compel him to pursue whatever is favourable to tazkiyah and totally refrain from anything which goes against it. Sincerity is a guarantee that a person will certainly reach the stage of tazkiyah.

Tazkiyah–A Psychological Act

The attainment of tazkiyah is not possible through any kind of verbal repetition, neither is it related to any kind of physical exercise. Tazkiyah is wholly a psychological act and can be attained only at that level.

A psychological act means an act at the intellectual level. The human mind is at the centre of all kinds of human development. It is in fact the mind which is the deciding factor in shaping the human personality. The non-purified personality and the purified personality are both products of the mind.

It is a positive intellectual development which is actually required for tazkiyah. That is, one has to develop one's conscious mind to such an extent that it may become discriminating, it may convert negative thoughts into positive thoughts, it may have glimpses of the Creator in His creation and may discover spiritual aspects in material events.

It may reject Satan's temptations, it may rise above the temptations of the self, it may distance itself from fruitless actions, it may make out its real well-wishers, it may accept advice, even if that be against its nature, it may develop anti-self thinking, and be able to set the goal of spirituality for itself, rising above material goals. One who thinks along these lines will become Hereafter-oriented.

All these developments take place at the psychological level, being the result of deep thinking. One who cannot engage in deep thinking will never attain high levels of tazkiyah. The process of tazkiyah can be initiated only in one who is capable of deep thought. Tazkiyah, in fact, is another name for psychological purification. First of all, tazkiyah is performed at the psychological level and only then is it possible for tazkiyah to be achieved at the level of the whole human existence.

The Importance of Positive Psychology

Four thousand years ago, Prophet Ibrāhīm settled his wife Hājar and his son Ismāʿīl in the desert of Arabia and returned to Syria. Later, when Ismāʿīl grew up he married a woman of the Jurhum tribe. After some time had elapsed, Ibrāhīm visited them and found only Ismāʿīl's wife at home. The woman complained of living in very difficult conditions. Prophet Ibrāhīm asked her to deliver the following message to Ismāʿīl, "Replace your doorway."

Ismāʿīl later divorced his wife and married another woman. After some time, Prophet Ibrāhīm came back to meet his family. Ismāʿīl was away and his new wife, rather than have any complaints or grudges was thankful for everything. On hearing this, Prophet Ibrāhīm said to her, "When Ismāʿīl comes home convey my message to him, 'Retain your doorway.'" (Ṣaḥīḥ al-Bukhārī, Hadith No. 3364)

Prophet Ibrāhīm had settled his family in the desert, so that in this natural environment a new generation would arise which would take up the message of God and spread it throughout the world. This incident concerning Prophet Ibrāhīm shows that the individuals required for this great task must above all have the quality of possessing a positive psychology, and have no propensity to complain. This shows what is of the utmost importance in the process of tazkiyah: that a person cease to complain and give utterance to grievances and that he become a positive thinker in the full sense, in spite of having every cause for complaint. Negative thinking is a killer of tazkiyah, whereas positive thinking is the most essential condition for tazkiyah. A person who indulges in negative thinking becomes subject to Satan. On the contrary, a person who engages in positive thinking lives in the companionship of the angels, and it is a fact that tazkiyah cannot be attained without the help of the angels.

Introspection—The Basis of Tazkiyah

There is a saying of ʿUmar Fārūq, "Introspect yourself before you are subjected to introspection." (Sunan al-Tirmidhī, Hadith No. 2459) Introspection is the basis of tazkiyah. It does not come about through a training camp. No formal course can serve this purpose, nor will any repetition of certain words be of any help. The only way to tazkiyah is through introspection, that is, self-appraisal or reforming oneself, and by giving deep thought to how tazkiyah is to be attained.

Man is the only creature who has the capacity for conceptual thought. Indeed, man is defined as an animal capable of conceptual thought. You can shape wood, and you can mould iron, but man himself is not so malleable. Man is his own engineer or maker. If man is unwilling to submit to the influence of others, there is no one who can shape his personality. This is why introspection plays a role in man's personality development, or his tazkiyah.

The role of a teacher is solely to provide a strong incentive for engaging in tazkiyah. He should develop the thinking in a person that if he does not engage in self-purification and reform himself, he will be forever ruined; he has to undertake tazkiyah himself and whatever he has to do should be done today without waiting for tomorrow.

Man tends to find justification for all of his faults; he always finds some words to prove that he is in the right. It is necessary for one who wants to purify himself to root out this mentality once and for all. But this can be done only by the individual concerned, and not by anyone else.

How to Engage in Introspection?

The real source of self-purification is introspection, that is, thinking about oneself, analyzing one's words and deeds, or in other words, becoming one's own judge, by thinking against oneself and assessing oneself objectively. And no tazkiyah is possible without such introspection.

The most powerful feeling in an individual is that of egoism. This feeling is so intense that every person lives with the notion that he is all in all. This is a form of self-glorification. This kind of attitude should be anathema to seekers of tazkiyah. What a person should do is develop in himself anti-self thinking, so that he may stand up to criticism. This feeling was so intense in 'Umar ibn al-Khaṭṭāb that he said, "May God bless the man who sends me the gift of my shortcomings." (Sunan al-Dārimī, Athar No. 675)

This introspective mentality is born out of a discovery—that of one's own helplessness. The seeker of tazkiyah must discover the reality that his sense of 'I' exists only at the level of his own senses, or feelings. It does not exist in reality; he has no power over anything outside of his own feelings. He exercises no power in the matters of his life and death, the life support system, the divine court, and so on. When a person discovers his total powerlessness, the feeling of helplessness is necessarily born within him. It is this feeling of helplessness which compels one to engage in introspection and it is in this discovery that the real secret of tazkiyah lies.

Seeing a Test Paper in Advance

A true seeker of tazkiyah often finds clear guidance in the form of dreams. Through dreams he learns how to advance along his path, stage by stage. In this way, the seeker is able to make his choices with conviction as if blessed with special divine succour. It may be likened to a student having access to a test paper in advance. A seeker of tazkiyah is repeatedly faced with all kinds of questions. Suppose he has to take one of two options.

If he prays to God on such occasions, it is quite possible that God may accept his prayer and guide him—through a dream—which may lead him from doubts and hesitation to conviction.

Such kinds of dreams are undoubtedly one of God's great blessings. But if someone does not accept guidance, even after having the dream, then his case may be likened to a student who failed in his exams even after having advance knowledge of his test paper.

Tazkiyah is 50% concerned with the seeker and 50% with God. The seeker of tazkiyah ought constantly to pray to God. This prayer will become a means to associating him with God. He should perform istikhāra (two-unit prayers) before going to bed, asking God to give him guidance through a dream. Istikhāra is as if seeking God's counsel in his affairs. And one who does so consistently never goes astray. If God shows him a dream to solve his problem, then he should regard this as God having given him a preview of his paper. Indeed he has no other choice. One who is offered guidance by God to this extent, but who even then fails to accept His guidance would be committing an unpardonable crime. God will not accept any excuse from such a person and he will be deprived forever from establishing any contact with God.

Tazkiyah and Renunciation of the World

In later times one group adopted the path of renunciation of the world in order to attain tazkiyah. But disenchantment with the world is required in the psychological sense rather than in the practical sense. The world is inhabited by human beings; as such, renouncing the world is akin to renouncing people. A preacher of truth or a reformer cannot afford to abandon people on any pretext. Others may see people from other angles, but a preacher looks at people as potential seekers. In the eyes of a reformer, every human being is a seeker of the truth, be he rich or poor, a commoner or a VIP, ruler or ruled. Even if he is a rival or a tyrant, in the eyes of the reformer, he is a human being. And every sincere preacher's first desire is to convey the truth to him.

A reformer cannot afford to say that if someone enters from one gate, he will go out from another gate. He will instead say that the visitor is a seeker for him and, as such, he will meet him and convey the message of truth to him with wisdom.

Renouncing the world is, in fact, renouncing the seekers. Renouncing the world is, in effect, to go away from those to whom the preacher would normally want to convey the divine truth. A businessman can walk away from everything but he cannot walk away from his customers. In a similar way, a preacher can tolerate everything but he cannot tolerate going to a secluded place where there are no people who may be potential seekers of the truth. When he remains among people, he may be beset by certain problems, but he overlooks them because he cannot afford to break off his relations with them. Along with tazkiyah, daʿwa, or conveying the message of God to people, is an equally important goal for the believer. And if a believer is sincere it is not possible for him either to give up his efforts to attain tazkiyah or to give up his daʿwa activities.

Tazkiyah—An Act of Preparation

In the present material world, everyone is in need of some employment. Everyone wants a good job. That is why everyone prepares himself professionally to meet the demands of the job market. One who fails to do so will be a failure all his life.

The same is true of the world Hereafter. But its exigencies are of a much more pressing nature. The world Hereafter is a world of divine activity of a very high order. In the Hereafter only that person will succeed who readies himself spiritually in this present world with the thought of the Hereafter in his mind. One who fails to prepare oneself appropriately in this world will be a failure in the Hereafter.

All this relates to competence. One type of competence works in this world, while another type of competence will avail in the Hereafter. In this world, a source other than God may work but, in the Hereafter, God alone will be of any avail. In this world making one's own self one's sole concern is advantageous but, in the Hereafter, it is making God one's sole concern which will be of benefit.

Tazkiyah means preparing oneself with regard to the Hereafter, that is, developing in oneself those qualities which will benefit one in the Hereafter. The way of tazkiyah is to activate one's thinking. One way to do this is to identify such incidents in your life when you were going to be plunged into some great trouble but you were saved by the special succour of God.

It is a must for the seeker of tazkiyah to recall such incidents repeatedly in order to refresh his mind of how, when he had reached the very brink of destruction, he was saved by the special intervention of God. He should keep remembering every graphic detail of these incidents and beseech God thus: "O God, You have repeatedly saved me from the horrible consequences of my actions in the life of this world. In the same way, save me from the horrible punishment of the Hereafter."

Another approach to this matter is to remember your shortcomings, your mistakes and awaken in yourself a feeling of repentance. If you feel that in any matter you were 99% right and you were wrong by only 1%, then on such occasions, you should forget the 99% and exaggerate the 1% to the point where you begin to feel that you were 100% wrong. This will awaken the feeling of repentance in you. You will shudder in the fear of God and will turn to Him in prayer and seek His forgiveness.

There is nothing mysterious about tazkiyah. It is a known process, that is, thinking repeatedly about all aspects of self-purification. Tazkiyah is always the result of an intellectual awakening, rather than the result of some mysterious miracle. The more one thinks about this matter, the more one will be able to attain a state of self-purification. Tazkiyah is a conscious process in the full sense. And hoping to achieve it without undergoing this conscious process is just wishful thinking. It will never become a reality.

Tazkiyah—A Means of Reaching God

Man is the creation and God is his Creator. As such, it is human nature that he should come close to God to the ultimate extent. But various things, such as pride, negative thinking, etc., separate man from God. Tazkiyah aims at thoroughly purifying one of such negative feelings. The moment one detaches oneself from things other than God, one instantly feels that one has come as close to one's Creator as it is humanly possible to come. One begins to experience the presence of God all around one.

When an individual discovers God as His Benefactor, then quite naturally a fountain of love for God wells up in his soul. Then he becomes the embodiment of the reality described thus in the Quran:

"Those who believe love God most." (2:165).

The Quran enjoins self-prostration as being necessary for nearness to the Creator:

"Prostrate yourself and come closer to God." (96:19)

What is this self-prostration? It is, in fact, the obeisance made by one who is filled with the love and fear of God: with these intense feelings, he falls prostrate before his Lord—this kind of prostration is as if a divine ascent for the believer.

The Purpose of Tazkiyah

Chapter 39 of the Quran describes the people of Paradise thus: "Those who fear their Lord will be led in groups towards Paradise. When they reach it, its gate will be opened, and its keepers will say to them, 'Peace be upon you. You have done well, enter Paradise and dwell in it forever,' and they will say, 'Praise be to God who has fulfilled His promise to us and made us the inheritors of this land, letting us settle in the Garden wherever we want.' How excellent is the reward of those who labour! You shall see the angels circling about the throne, glorifying their Lord with praise. And judgement will have been passed in justice on all and it will be said, 'Praise be to God, Lord of the Universe!'" (39:73–75)

The invocation, 'Praise be to God, the Lord of the Universe' is a part of the first chapter in relation to this present world, while in Chapter 39, these words relate to the world of the Hereafter. This shows that what is truly desired of a person is that he should lead a life of remembrance and glorification of God. What is desirable in this world is equally desirable in the next world. The actual aim of tazkiyah is to bring into existence such purified souls as may glorify God and become a part of the life Hereafter.

One task assigned to man in this present world was to bring civilization into existence—a task performed by man on a very large scale. This journey of civilization began from the Stone Age and was taken to the heights of the electronic age. It gained enormous momentum with the discovery of the laws of nature. But what, in effect, happened was that a right was mixed with a wrong. After overcoming the forces of nature, man became insolent and encouraged anarchy in the name of freedom. That is why on the Day of Judgement God will select righteous people who will be given the opportunity to establish a divine civilization. This is the reality which finds expression in this verse of the Quran: "My righteous servants shall inherit the earth." (21:105)

It is a fact that human life is a journey of realization, which extends from this world to the Hereafter. In this world, the journey of realization takes place on a very limited scale. On the contrary, in the Hereafter the journey of realization will know no limits. However, this journey may be successfully undertaken only by one who has proved to be a deserving candidate of Paradise by having purified his soul. The Quran tells us that God's words are so innumerable that even if the seven seas were doubled and all these seas were turned into ink and all the trees of the world were turned into pens, even then the ink would not suffice to write down all of God's words. The Quran expresses it thus: "If all the trees on earth were pens, and the sea [were] ink, with seven [more] seas added to it, the words of God would not be exhausted." (31:27)

This is not simply a statement but a command by God Almighty to be followed by believers. This means that believers ought to discover the words of God and thus continue discovering God's wonders and increasing their realization of God. The first verse of the Quran, "Praise be to God, the Lord of the Universe," (1:2) is the beginning and not the end. This verse announces the beginning of the journey of realization in this world. At another place this verse appears with reference to the world Hereafter: "It will be said, 'Praise be to God, Lord of the Universe.'" (39:75)

This second verse tells us the ultimate stage of God-realization, which will continue for all eternity in the most favourable environment of the Hereafter.

In the first stage of realization the scientists of the 19th and 20th centuries have played a very great role in providing a scientific framework for the realization of God.

As we learn from the Quran, in the life Hereafter, the believers will be supported by the angels in their journey of realization: "We are your companions in this life and in the Hereafter." (41:31)

The Criterion of Tazkiyah

The Quran states:

> *"He who purifies it (soul) will indeed be successful and he who corrupts it is sure to fail." (91:9–10).*

We learn from this verse of the Qur'ān that purification (tazkiyah) means saving one's God-given personality from corruption or defilement. As for man's nature, he is born with it. Every human being comes into this world with the purified personality desirable by God. But in leading his life in this world, he never ceases to corrupt his God-given nature. In modern terminology this is called environmental or societal conditioning.

In this respect, the criterion of purification is for a person to learn about his fall from grace through introspection. And on the principle of self-reform he should rehabilitate himself and return to the natural state bestowed upon him by his Creator. The purified personality in other words is restored to pristine virtue. One who purifies himself in this way is the one who will be held deserving of entry into Paradise in the Hereafter.

What is the criterion of tazkiyah? It is that one becomes so in tune with the divine way of thinking and the divine way of life that one feels that one is being guided by the voice of one's own nature. Without any hesitation one should be willing to accept this, even if it runs counter to one's cherished desires.

The real aim of tazkiyah is attachment to God. This is the whole truth. To put it another way, tazkiyah enables one to focus so totally on God that one becomes free of all other considerations, save devotion to God. Tazkiyah enables one to make God the centre of one's attention in the complete sense.

Making God one's sole concern is no simple matter. It is akin to bringing about a total revolution in one's psyche. One who experiences such a revolution takes God as the Giver in the full sense, and regards himself as the taker in the full sense. His thinking becomes God-oriented: his feelings are centred entirely on God. His words and deeds reflect the divine culture. Modesty grows within him, he becomes a man cut to size. His heart is full of well-wishing instead of hatred for others. Instead of becoming haughty and insolent, he becomes modest.

His attitude to others is submissive rather than insolent. In all matters, he owns up to his own mistakes rather than blame others. He begins to prefer remaining silent rather than be talkative. Instead of occupying the front seat, he prefers to take the back seat.

Before uttering a single word, he gives thought to whether his words in the presence of God will be accepted or rejected. In private, he is as cautious as he is in public.

Tazkiyah and Remembrance of Death

For the process of Tazkiyah to go forward, the remembrance of death acts as a very powerful spur. The remembrance of death produces a sense of urgency in a person. Death reminds him of the fact that he cannot afford to procrastinate in his striving towards tazkiyah, a task which has to be undertaken today itself, for nobody knows for certain whether tomorrow will be the day of death or of life.

The concept of death reminds an individual of the moment when he will die, and that afterwards he will face a very grave situation. This moment of death has been described thus in the Quran: "The Day when mankind will stand before the Lord of the Universe." (83:6). This will be the day when angels will take a person before God. God, who knows everything, both open and hidden, will take him to account for all his words and deeds on earth. According to one tradition, man will on that day stand before God and his feet will not move until he has answered all the questions God will ask him. (Sunan al-Tirmidhī, Hadith No. 2416).

Remembering death means remembering the most delicate moment of one's life. An individual must keep thinking about the time—which is certainly going to come—when his eternal future will be decided.

Such thinking must certainly produce an upheaval. It is a fact that one who thinks about death in this manner will be extremely concerned about tazkiyah. He will try to the ultimate extent to attain tazkiyah from every aspect before death overtakes him, for then he will have reached a point where there is no time left for reform.

Towards Spiritual Civilization

It is desirable for a person to strive to discover the signs of God hidden in nature and to acknowledge God at the elevated level of God-realization. In this way, he brings into existence a Godly or divine civilization. In the present world, he has been given freedom for the purpose of being put to the test. But by misusing this freedom in this present world, he establishes a civilization which is non-spiritual in nature. But God wants a spiritual civilization: very soon this world will come to an end and will be replaced by a better world. (The Qur'ān, 42:36)

It is in this world, called the Hereafter that it would be possible, according to God's desired plan, to bring a high level of spiritual civilization into existence. Here it would be possible for an elevated level of God-realization to be attained. According to the will of the Lord, an ideal society will come into existence. It will be a perfect world where it will be possible for one to achieve fulfilment in every respect.

The aim of Tazkiyah is to find virtuous souls for this spiritual society or heavenly civilization of the future. Tazkiyah means that such upright individuals be prepared for this heavenly society as are well-adapted to living in this ideal world, whose thinking, conversation, habits, and tastes in every respect have that sublime character which is desired in the Hereafter for life in Paradise.

The present world has been created in order to prepare such individuals and it is this preparation which is called purification. This purification is brought about by one's own reflection and introspection. In that way, what we are going to experience in the society of Paradise is being experienced again and again in this present world. On this subject, the angels are preparing a person's record of his relations and his dealings with others, and what kind of response he has given in different situations, heavenly or non-heavenly, spiritual or non-spiritual, right or wrong, responsible or irresponsible. It is on the basis of this record of those who have given the desired response in this present world that candidates for Paradise will be selected.

It is these selected souls who will gain entry into the world of Paradise. And it is these people who will build a spiritual civilization. This is a process which will go on and on forever. Just as there is no limit to the words of God (31:27), similarly, there is no limit to this process of building a spiritual civilization.

Spiritual Progress

What is spiritual progress? Spiritual progress is another name for a spiritual awakening in one's internal personality. Material food makes one's physical body healthy. Similarly, the spiritual existence of a person becomes healthy through such refinements as are called spiritual divine food. (The Qur'ān, 20:131)

It was July 16, 2004. It was a very hot day in Delhi. The light went off for a long period in the afternoon. The ceiling fan stopped. I sat in my room in that heat of July. For a long time I stayed in this condition. Finally the light came back on and the fan started functioning.

It was a sudden experience. The moment the fan started rotating the body cooled down. It seemed as though the hour of distress had come to an end and comfort had been restored. At that time, I was reminded of two traditions of the Prophet of Islam in which it is spelled out that the world for a believer is a place of great difficulty or distress. (Ṣaḥīḥ Muslim, Hadith No. 2956) But when the believer leaves this world after death, he will find himself all of a sudden in the gardens of Paradise. (Sunan Ibn Mājah, Hadith No. 4262) The difficult worldly life of afflictions will all of a sudden come to an end, and exactly at the same time the phase of comfort of the afterlife will begin.

When I had this experience, the latent spiritual feelings hidden in nature were awakened. A material event had transformed into a spiritual event. These words came to my lips:

> "May God do the same for me when the time comes for
> me to leave the world."

Then it should be a moment when all of a sudden it is akin to leaving a period of affliction and entering into a period of comfort.

Spirituality is indeed an intellectual journey, a journey which takes one from materialism to a world of meaning. This journey takes place at the internal level. Others are not apparently able to see or understand this journey, but the traveller feels it deeply. Spirituality makes one a human being. The person whose life is devoid of spirituality, is no different from the animals.

What Is Introspection?

According to a tradition, the second Caliph 'Umar Fārūq observed:

> *"Reckon yourself before being reckoned, measure yourself before being measured." (Musannaf Ibn Abī Shaybah, Athar No. 34459).*

This adage enshrines a very important principle for self-reform. If a person adheres to this principle, it will ensure his reformation and his purification.

What does introspection mean? Introspection, in fact, is a way of discovering one's mistakes. An individual repeatedly makes mistakes and deviates from the straight path of truth. It is discovering this point of deviation from the truth which is called introspection.

When a person discovers the starting point of this deviation, he can easily reform himself, but remaining in error for a long period of time makes it almost impossible to rectify one's mistakes. That is why a person must be very careful to mend his ways sooner rather than later.

The reason is that, in the beginning, being in error is a matter of deviation. Later on it becomes a matter of conditioning. At the time of the first deviation, a person's conscience alerts him to his wrongdoing. But if he fails to reform himself with this initial warning, this deviation from the truth gradually ceases to be alien to his thinking and ultimately takes a permanent place in his unconscious mind. When this happens, rectifying one's mistakes becomes almost impossible.

The Building of a Positive Personality

Jean Jacques Rousseau (1712–1778) was a well known democratic thinker of France. He was the upholder of the rule of the people rather than the rule of monarchy. He begins his famous book, Social Contract, with this sentence:

"Man was born free, but I find him in chains."

But man is faced with another, perhaps more serious problem, and that is, conditioning. All men and women are influenced by their immediate environment. Because of this, their minds become conditioned, as a result of which they are deficient in right thinking. A person is not therefore able to think realistically. In view of this problem, we need to rephrase Rousseau's dictum: Man was created on the pattern of divine nature, but I see him psychologically conditioned.

When a child is born out of his mother's womb, he appears to be the embodiment of innocence. It seems as if an angel has taken the form of a human body. At the time of birth, man's mind is pure. His thinking is as natural as it ought to be.

But man is a social animal. He has to spend his whole life in society along with other people. Because of this, he continues to receive external influences at all times. This is known as conditioning. This influence goes on increasing until a time comes when he becomes conditioned to the ultimate degree.

When one reaches adulthood, i.e. the age of maturity, every man and woman must make an effort to understand this conditioning, and by de-conditioning one's mind, one should take oneself back to the natural state in which one was born. Instead of being an artificial person, one should become a man or woman whose nature is in its pure, pristine state.

The conditioning of the environment acts as an artificial veil over the real man's eyes. The human personality is like an onion. Inside the onion there is a kernel-like structure of the size of a pea. Over this internal 'kernel', there are a number of external covers wrapped around it. When one removes these covers one-by-one, the inner 'kernel' will be revealed. The same is true also of a human being. Because of the environment, the human personality becomes shrouded in artificial veils. Once these are removed, one's real personality will come into the open.

De-conditioning is another name for removing the external veils covering the human personality. For one who is a seeker of truth, it is incumbent upon him to remove all the artificial veils by means of de-conditioning so that his real personality may come to the fore.

According to religious teachings, as a human being is God's special creation, he is born with a divine personality. As to his inner existence, he is a perfect, complete personality. The essential condition for eternal success is that a person must first of all guard the personality he was born with and that he should strictly adhere to the natural state in which he has been created by God. De-conditioning is another name for this struggle entailed in self-building.

The search for truth or the discovery of truth are both the acts of a positive personality. It is, in actual fact, a positive personality which serves as the proper soil in which to grow the noble urge to search for the truth. And it is a positive personality which, because of its sound thinking, ultimately reaches the stage of discovering the truth.

Spirituality: Converting Material Provision into Spiritual Provision

I was once asked to explain the concept of spirituality in Islam and what, from the Islamic viewpoint, the method was of attaining spirituality. I said that the word "spirituality" (or rūḥāniyyāt) began to be used later in the history of Islam. In the Qur'ān the word used for it is rabbāniyyāt (3:79), meaning the virtue of being God-oriented.

It is generally believed that there is only one way of finding spirituality and that is through renunciation. But that is not true. What we achieve by renouncing the world is not spirituality but mysticism (rahbāniyyāt) and, according to a tradition, mysticism is not desirable in Islam. (Musnad Aḥmad, Hadith No. 25893)

Rūḥāniyyāt or rabbāniyyāt means one's inner personality may acquire godly qualities by becoming immersed in thoughts of God and the Hereafter. This level of spirituality is produced after an intellectual revolution rather than by renouncing the material world. This is an act of intellectual rather than physical renunciation. According to the Qur'ān, the way to this intellectual renunciation is tawassum, meaning the learning of lessons.

Such spirituality can be found through an intellectual awakening which in the Qur'ān is called abundant remembrance of God (dhikr-i kathīr) (62:10).

This abundant remembrance of God is not simply a matter of repeating words. It is, in fact, an intellectual act of seeing God's signs in material things and learning lessons related to the Hereafter from material experiences. This spiritual or divine aspect is hidden in all worldly things. Spirituality enables one engaged in material or worldly activities to see the divine signs. Spirituality can be attained neither by renouncing the world nor by the repetition of certain words. Spirituality can be attained only by one who has the intellectual ability to convert material provision into spiritual food.

A Deadly Habit

Life is a straight path, and one who keeps to this straight path will be bound to reach the destination of success. Distraction is the only thing which can act as an obstacle in this journey, that is, distraction by things, which are not related to the straight path, and which cause one to deviate from the straight path.

The Forbidden Tree in Paradise was in fact a sign of such distraction. In the very beginning, man was told that he was settled there for the purpose of putting him to the test. There will be many "Forbidden Trees" in life which will be sources of distraction. If you can save yourself from the deviation caused by these "Forbidden Trees", you will certainly be successful in reaching your destination.

There are many forms of distraction. If a person gives serious thought to this, he will be able to understand that he is becoming distracted and can save himself. But the worst form of distraction is that which becomes a habit in one's daily life. Once a man is addicted to this, he starts doing that same thing without thinking about it and it becomes a part of an unconscious process.

In present times, many new addictions have found a place in one's life. People, for example, are addicted to the internet, the telephone, the mobile phone, Facebook and so on. People have become so addicted to all these things that they cannot live without them. Such habits have progressively caused great deprivation to a person. God has granted an individual a mind to think of important things, discover and understand important realities but everyone is too busy with the cell phone and so engaged in trivialities that one has no time to devote to more important issues.

The Method of De-conditioning

Everyone is born in an environment which exerts an influence on him. This is a process of conditioning. This is true of everyone without exception, and it is a problem for everyone, because such conditioning causes one to deviate from nature. That is why it is essential that everyone de-condition himself and return to his original nature.

There is only one way to decondition oneself, and that is by introspection. This entails rigorously continuing to engage in the act of self-reform. There are two ways to do this. One is to tolerate the harsh criticism of others, that is, accepting with an open mind any adversarial evaluation of one's thinking and conduct without taking this to heart; one should engage without delay in one's self-reassessment.

Another method of deconditioning is self-criticism. That is, one should look at himself like an enemy. He should assess himself morning and evening. He should keenly feel his mistakes and then introspect. He should engage in a merciless hammering of his ego. In no matter should he make concessions to himself. Instead of blaming others, he should always first blame himself. He should become such a severe critic of himself that it is as if he is trying to put an end to himself.

These are the only two methods of de-conditioning oneself. Either one accepts the harsh criticism of others or one becomes a harsh critic of oneself. Those who always want sweet, polite words from others, and those who always make concessions to themselves will always remain in a conditioned state and will never be able to de-condition themselves.

Spirituality Without Intellectual Revolution

Spirituality has always been a subject of interest. It is known by many names, for instance, mysticism, meditation, sufism, etc. For thousands of years great activities have been engaged in to attain spirituality. But these activities have not yielded any real results. Despite all man's efforts and struggle, what has been gained is ecstasy rather than the intellectual development which was desired from these activities.

The truth is that since ancient times people have come to believe that the human mind is the centre of thinking, while the human heart is the centre of emotions and feelings, and because spirituality has come to be regarded as deriving from emotions and sentiments, people always believed in heart-based spirituality. Because of this supposition, the theory was developed that a person's heart was the source of all spiritual treasures, and by awakening these feelings and emotions hidden in the heart, one could attain spirituality.

But, in present times, scientific research has found this supposition to be baseless. Now it has been learnt with certainty that the only centre of thoughts and feelings is the human mind. As far as the heart is concerned, it is only a muscular organ which keeps up the circulation of blood by contracting and dilating.

This is why, for several thousand years, what man has found as a result of great spiritual struggle is merely ecstasy rather than any intellectual development. This kind of spirituality, in fact, is an unreasoning form of emotionalism rather than any spiritual development in the real sense.

As we know, ecstasy is another name for rapture, whereas the greatest evidence of man's spirituality is that he possesses a mind which is capable of thinking. Indeed, if spirituality is to be given credence, it must be found to exist at the level of the mind. Just as all the material progress made in human history has resulted from harnessing this thinking faculty to superior ends, so also spiritual progress needs to be made through intellectual activity.

Spirituality is, in fact, a sublime state of realization of the truth. It has nothing in common with some vague state of ecstasy. It follows that true spirituality is that state which can be attained at the level of the mind rather than at the level of the heart.

Due to a lack of awareness of this reality, man has largely remained deprived of true spirituality throughout the entirety of human history. What he regarded as spirituality was not spirituality. It was due to this lack of awareness of the truth on his part that he failed to progress towards true spirituality. There is no tragedy greater than this in all of human history.

Chapter 03

GOD-ORIENTED LIFE

Two Arrangements

God has created man with special blessings, which are basically of two kinds. One of them is called the "best of mould" in the Qur'ān (95:4). The other blessing has been thus referred to in the Qur'ān:

"He has given you all that you asked of Him." (14:34)

The "best of mould" has also been referred to in the Qur'ān as "best form" (40:64). This means that man has been granted a perfect physique.

The human body is regulated, moreover, by a number of organs, which enable sight, hearing, breathing, speech, digestion, blood circulation and movement. All of these are essential for the survival of human life and, if these systems were ever disturbed or deteriorated and became non-functional, human life would come to an end. Other blessings which have been provided in the outside world, external to human existence, make up the life support system. They include the system of light and heat, the supply of oxygen, rains, agriculture, etc. Human life depends for its continuance upon both the internal organ support system and the external life support system.

A deeper knowledge of these natural processes opens the door to the realization of God. As a result, profound feelings of thankfulness are engendered, which give birth to all manner of positive qualities like modesty, seriousness, willingness to accept the truth, and so on.

The Miracle of Creation

Man is a masterpiece of the creative power of God. In this vast universe no creature like man exists. This has been mentioned in the Qur'ān in different ways. We learn from the Qur'ān that

> *"We have honoured the children of Adam ... and exalted them above many of Our creatures." (17.70).*

In the same vein God says:

> *"We have indeed created man in the best of mould."*
> *(95:4)*

Furthermore:

> *"He shaped you, formed you well, and provided you with good things." (40:64)*

A human being undoubtedly is the greatest masterpiece of divine creation. If you apprehend your existence in this way, you will have a great surge of feelings of acknowledgement of God. In your inner self, you will feel that God's blessings upon you are so great that to describe it, no human words are sufficient. This discovery will give you a great point of reference for prayer. You will call out: "O God, you showered me with such great blessings in this world, will you deprive me of Your blessings in the world Hereafter? Will You consign Your masterpiece to hellfire?"

But it is strange how people have failed to recognize themselves as masterpieces of divine creation. Everyone attributes all greatness to himself—as a matter of personal achievement. As a result, everyone lives in and for his own self. Everyone takes the high ground of pride. Everyone, consciously or unconsciously, thinks that he is all in all. There are other types of people who are given to the cult of personalities. When they see greatness in their saints or gurus, they attribute it to those human beings and then start worshipping or revering them. The greatness that they should have attributed to the Creator they have attributed instead to the creature. As a result, they have stooped to the worship of the creation rather than the Creator.

Control Over the Universe

The words of the 2nd verse of the Qur'ān: "Praise be to God, the Lord of the Universe (1:2)" are in actual fact, a person's spontaneous utterance when he observes the universe. Telescopic observation tells us that the universe is, to an unimaginable extent, vast and majestic. Moreover, microscopic studies tell us that the unobservable universe is as majestic as the observable universe. In spite of all progress made by humanity, man has not yet succeeded in apprehending either the vastness or the grandeur of the universe.

This vast and unfathomable universe is continuously in motion. At every moment, extremely meaningful events are taking place. Further study tells us that this vast universe is totally faultless. The universe can continually remain in a faultless state, only when there is not even the most minute alteration in its system. Even the tiniest deviation in the universe can disturb its entire system.

Modern studies tell us that in spite of the universe being vast to an unimaginable extent, it is entirely harmonious in its functioning. That is because it is completely controlled by a single force. All its parts are perfectly connected with one another.

On seeing this universal harmoniousness, scientists find it astonishing. They do not know how to explain this extraordinary feature. This perfect harmony in the universe is a proof that it is functioning under an All-Powerful Creator. Had this not been so, the whole universe would be reduced to ultimate chaos. This perfect harmony prevailing in the universe is possible only because its Controller possesses the attribute of Omnipotence.

The Beginning of Realization

The Qur'ān states:

*"We have created man into a life of toil and trial. Does
he think then that no one has power over him?" (90:4–5)*

The law of the present world is so designed that man must inevitably undergo hardships. No one is exempt from this general law. This fact shows how helpless a human being is. In this world, it is only the Creator who is Almighty, All-Powerful. This contradistinction is final. No one is exempted from it (that is, God is All-Powerful and man is totally powerless).

The Qur'ān states:

"Every human being is bound to taste death." (3:185).

It is a historical fact that whoever is born into this world has to die after a limited period of time.

The incidence of death bespeaks one's helplessness. This event proves that helplessness is man's lot in life. So far as power is concerned, none but the Creator has power. Both these experiences, for men and women alike, are of a proven finality. In this way, everyone can discover, in the light of his or her personal experiences, that he or she is in a position of total helplessness and, as compared to man, the Creator is Omnipotent.

This discovery is the beginning of realization. For one who makes this discovery, the journey towards the path of realization has been well and truly initiated. Subsequently, all other things, which are desirable in the divine way will become part of his or her life. This realization is like an intellectual revolution in that it colours one's entire life in the hue of God. (2:138)

Mind and Religion

Chapter 38 of the Qur'ān has this to say:

*"This is a blessed Book which We sent down to you
[Muḥammad], for people to ponder over its messages,
and for those with understanding to take heed." (38:29)*

From this verse we learn that the Qur'ān is not meant merely for verbal recitation: it is for the reader to make use of his mind and reflect upon and ponder over its verses in order to learn the lessons hidden in the verses or between the lines.

There are many traditions of the Prophet as regards the importance of the mind. The wording of one of these is:

*"Everything has a pillar and the pillar of a believer is
his reason or mind ('aql)." (Musnad al-Ḥārith, Hadith
No. 840)*

There is another ḥadīth of relevance in which the Prophet of Islam observed:

*"Every verse of the Qur'ān has an external aspect or form
and an internal essence or inner aspect." (Musnad Abū
Yaʿlā, Hadith No. 5149)*

The apparent meaning of the verses is understood by just reading the verses, but the deeper meaning can be arrived at only by employing reason, and pondering upon what one reads. The reader, thus, reaches the deeper level of the meaning of the verses by reflection. This deeper realization of the Qur'ān produces sublime feelings of faith in one. While without making use of reason, one arrives at a form of religion which is superficial. It is only by making use of reason that the seeker can find the true kernel of religion.

Why should there be Trials?

When God's servant calls to his Lord, and if he is dear to God, He says,

In this tradition, the word 'voice' is not only a matter of utterance, but has a wider connotation. This voice is of one who has experienced trial according to the law of nature. His heart has been deeply affected by this experience, which has brought to him a storm of divine ideas. Through it he has discovered humility and the greatness of God. As a result, a new storm emerges in his spirit.

On such occasions, the words that come out of the mouth of a believer are unique, special words expressive of the glory of God. A believer becomes the envy of the whole universe at that particular moment. He remembers God in such a way that the earth and heaven also failed to do so. This is the highest form of divine remembrance of a creative nature.

Trial is a divine experience for a believer, leading to an increase in his sensitivity. At that time, the words of prayer that come out of his mouth in remembering God, are not a mere repetition of words but, a form of religious creativity. He calls God in such divine spiritual words of which he himself had no prior knowledge. At that time, the words he utters are so noble that God himself loves to hear his voice.

The Essence of Faith

As we know, faith has its own special flavour or innate characteristic quality. It is reported in a tradition that one who is willing to make God his Lord will savour that essence of faith. (Ṣaḥīḥ Muslim, Hadith No. 34) Tastes vary considerably from each other. For example, God has created a number of fruits, each with its own individual flavour. For instance, the fig has a different taste from a date. Grapes have a taste not found in apples. A mango has a taste quite distinct from that of a banana. Each fruit has its own unique taste. When anyone eats a piece of fruit, he savours this individual taste. The same holds true of the essence of faith. For believers, God has bestowed upon happiness a taste which is absent from sorrow. Affluence has an innate quality missing from poverty. Health has a taste which illness does not have. The same goes for difficulty and ease. Moreover, faith may be better savoured in anonymity rather than in repute. Power has a taste which powerlessness can never have on a parallel with strength vis-à-vis helplessness.

However, it depends upon a man's awareness whether he can savour faith in different situations. The ability to savour faith is not an unconditional bestowal. It comes with the condition that one fully understands what is meant by living faith.

Just as it is only one with fully sensitive taste buds who will be able to discriminate between the tastes of different fruits, it is only one who is alive in his sense of faith, and also continually revivifies it, who will be able to appreciate the taste of faith in different sets of circumstances. On the contrary one who allows his sense of faith to become blunted, may experience different types of situations, but he will never be able to savour the sacred taste immanent in them. Even if living in the garden of faith, he will never know the divine aroma of faith.

Man–An Exceptional Creature

A tradition of the Prophet of Islam reported in books of ḥadīth reads:

> *"God created Adam in His own image." (Ṣaḥīḥ al-Bukhārī, Hadith No. 6227)*

This does not mean that man is like God in physical appearance. It means that God has in a limited way granted to man those divine attributes which exist in perfect form in God's being.

In the entire universe a human being is an exceptional creature. His is a living existence. He is the only creature who has been granted a complete personality. He thinks, sees, hears, carries out planned action and can enjoy a multitude of things by using his five senses. All these are exceptional qualities which are granted only to man out of all the creatures in the entire universe.

Man has been given these exceptional gifts so that he may engage himself in an exceptional task. This exceptional task is to discover and apprehend the Creator at a conscious level. In this way, the Almighty Lord of the Universe has given man the opportunity to discover Him at the level of realization. He may see God while He Himself is unseen. He may render himself powerless before God; in spite of having power; he may surrender himself before God without any compulsion.

He is blessed in having been given the ability to convert the entire world of nature into spiritual provision for himself, for he has to develop himself intellectually by awakening his consciousness. When he does so, he finds truth at the level of personal discovery; the realization of God comes to him as he bows in self-prostration. Then he has to develop his personality to such a degree of moral refinement that he may be held deserving of finding a place in the vicinity of Almighty God, that is, Paradise. Those who fail to develop such a personality are worthless in the eyes of God.

Three Levels of Development

A tradition is recorded in different books of ḥadīth. In the words of Ṣaḥīḥ Muslim, Abū Hurayrah narrated that the Prophet of Islam said: "Man is like metal—like silver and gold. One who was better in the days of ignorance (that is, prior to Islam) is also better in Islam, if he can develop a deeper understanding in Islam." (Ṣaḥīḥ Muslim, Hadith No. 2638 b)

In this tradition, the stages of a person's intellectual development are explained. The first intellectual level is the one on which human beings are born. The second intellectual level is that which one attains by one's own efforts. The third level is that of realization of God. By reaching the level of realization, the individual can achieve the final destination of his intellectual development. That is, the level the other name of which is Islam.

In this sense, an individual's example is like the metal. Iron is mined from the ground in the form of ores i.e., in its original state. After that, it is melted and purified. Then it takes the form of iron. Next, it passes through the industrial process of combining it with carbon to form the alloy steel. After that it can be made into machines, tools, etc. That is, in the first step it is an ore, in the second step iron and in the third and final step it is steel.

This is the case of the human being. A person's birth is like his coming to the outer world from his natural mine. After that, he grows up, thinks and undergoes the stages of getting an education and training. In this way he reaches the stage of maturity and becomes a complete person. This is the middle phase of human life. After this, if a person uses his reason along right lines, he is able to reach the level of realization of God.

This is the stage when a person who is born into this world may reach the heights of humanity and may attain the state of one who has realized God ('ārif bi-llāh). Every individual has an inborn personality bestowed upon him by God. Initially everyone is equal. It is only later, with the development of human potential, that differences arise.

Some achieve a higher level of development than others; the highest level is that of God-realization. There is a tradition which says: "To God, the young believer is better than the old one, and that everyone is good, that is, there is good in everyone. Take those things which are beneficial for you, seek help from God and be humble. And if anything thwarts you, don't say:

> *'I wish I had done such a thing differently'. Say rather: 'It was according to God's plan.'" (Ṣaḥīḥ Muslim, Hadith No. 2664).*

If a person himself feels inferior, he should not lose heart because he may possess hitherto unsuspected qualities. An individual should discover his own potential and live his life accordingly. During any struggle, if he faces problems he should understand that there may also be positive advantages in negative experiences. A person should learn positive lessons from his negative experiences. He should not lose hope in any situation to the point of feeling victimized. He must rather learn to think positively.

In this way, he will continue to develop his personality. By introspection, he can reverse wrong conditioning. By awakening his consciousness, he will develop his personality in such a way that he has the capacity to accept the truth. He must follow this prayer said by the Prophet Muḥammad:

> *"O God! Show me the truth as it is and give me the strength to follow it. And show me falsity as it is, and protect me from it." (Tafsīr Ibn Kathīr, vol. 1, p. 427)*

And

> *"O God! Show me things as they are.' (Tafsīr al-Rāzī, vol. 1, p. 119)*

One who thinks positively may be described as having a developed personality. Wise is one who builds up such a personality. As far as everyday experience is concerned, God gives natural gifts to all of us equally. But, subsequently it is the duty of the human being to turn himself into a developed personality. It is like using machinery to convert the ore found in nature into steel.

The next development is based on this process of self-preparation. The self-taught introspect continuously and analyze their mistakes in order to de-condition themselves. They are the ones who have at all costs converted ore into steel. They are the ones who avoid such things as create obstacles to their personality development, for example, ego, pride, envy, anger and revenge.

In short, they are the ones who, having analyzed themselves completely, have been able to discover God and accept Him totally and unconditionally. This they have done by the grace of God.

Purification (Tazkiyah) is compulsory for all men and women. This entails their resisting and overcoming the influences of their environment which we describe as conditioning. In consonance with one's feelings and desires people develop certain habits. Consciously or unconsciously under the influence of their interests, they become conditioned in such habits. All these things create obstacles to their leading a spiritual life. To overcome these obstacles, an individual has to become his own guide. He must identify his mistakes, and apply to himself the process of rigorous de-conditioning. This is a prerequisite for purification. Without this, no one can be genuinely purified. No one can get entry into Paradise, without self-purification.

Those who have been successful in engaging in these processes, discover the truth. They have been mentioned in the Qur'ān as "soul at peace" (89:27). They are the ones who fell in line with the creation plan of God and who developed in themselves the desired personality according to His creation plan. These are the ones who will be rewarded by God and will gain entry into Paradise.

The Veil of Satan

The following is a part of a long tradition:

> *"Satans keep hovering over the eyes of human beings, so that they may not reflect upon the divine signs scattered all over the earth and the heavens. Had it not been so, they would certainly see divine marvels." (Musnad Aḥmad, Hadith No. 8625)*

The universe around us is called nature in scientific terminology. Man comes across numerous events or phenomena in this vast world of nature. He sees and experiences them without learning any lesson from them. This verse of the Qur'ān applies to the unheeding:

> *"And there are many signs in the heavens and the earth that they pass by and give no heed to." (12:105)*

These events scattered in the universe are in fact divine signs: they serve as an introduction to the Creator in the form of His creation. If a person were to see with open eyes, he would observe the marvels of nature in these signs. But Satan puts such thoughts in man's mind as prevent him from seeing those events of nature from the right perspective. It is Satan who puts the thought in a person's mind that all those signs of nature are the result of the laws of cause and effect, happening automatically, rather than the result of divine power. Satan tries to stop man from looking at these events from the point of view of deriving lessons from them. He strives to make man look at them purely from the point view of material gain. Satan tries to make man take everything around him for granted and not ponder or reflect upon them. It is these Satanic whisperings which deprive man of the right realization of God and reality.

Humility–A Great Form of Worship

Tradition has it that every person is a sinner and the best one is he who repents for his sins, which is a great form of worship. This relates to God as well as human beings. When you acknowledge your wrongdoing before God, this is called 'repentance' or tawbah, and when in relation to human beings, repentance means admitting that one was wrong. (Sunan al-Tirmidhī, Hadith No. 2499)

A study of the lives of the Prophet's Companions reveals that they were truly and frequently repentant. There were many occasions when one of the Companions said that he had made a mistake and asked for forgiveness, even although in the purely legal sense, he had not made any kind of mistake. This was because they felt that they might have erred unintentionally.

Why was this so? It was because saying 'I was wrong' is in fact to establish one's humility. According to Islamic doctrine or belief, at all times the angels of God are near to every person. They are constantly noting down records of man's words and deeds. In such a situation, it is absolutely natural that a true believer will be extremely serious about the angels recording him as a humble person and not as a rebellious one.

This feeling is natural. It arises consciously or unconsciously, in everyone. Therefore, a believer does not like to appear as an arrogant person in the eyes of the angels. Even in the case where apparently he has not made a mistake, because of his humility, he often utters these words: "I was at fault", (I was in the wrong). By not admitting the mistake, rebellious emotions get the better of one. On the contrary, by admitting mistakes, one demonstrates his humility. Refusal to accept one's wrongdoings shows arrogance, whereas admitting one's mistakes is a sign of the true believer who has surrendered himself before the Lord.

What is Taqwā?

It is recorded in a tradition that 'Umar al-Fārūq once asked Ubayy ibn Ka'b what taqwā was. He replied,

> *"Have you ever passed by thorny bushes?" He said he had. Ubayy ibn Ka'b then asked, "What did you do then?" 'Umar al-Fārūq said that he had gathered up his clothes and cautiously kept away from the thorns, so as not to get entangled. Ubayy ibn Ka'b replied that that was taqwā. (Tafsīr Ibn Kathīr, vol. 1, p. 75)*

We learn the reality of taqwā from this tradition. Taqwā actually means that in this world, one should keep away from all kinds of trials and tribulations. It can be summed up in one phrase, a 'cautious approach'. At all times in the world there are different types of temptations, and great and small tribulations. In such conditions, the way of taqwā is for a person to keep sedulously away from all these and adopt a cautious approach on all occasions.

Two things are very important to be able to adhere to this path—sincerity and introspection. That is, to reflect upon everything very seriously and to introspect at all times. These two practices will act as a guarantee that one will continue to remain on the path of taqwā and will steer clear of non-godly paths which will lead to distraction.

Taqwā does not mean adopting some outward form of dress. It is mentioned in the tradition that taqwā relates to the heart. (Ṣaḥīḥ Muslim, Hadith No. 2864-a)

Those who reflect deeply on matters will be able to follow this path of taqwā. In reality, taqwā is the name of one's internal state. If a person is not God-conscious internally, no outward form or practice can grant him the status of a person imbued with taqwā. According to a ḥadīth, God does not see the outward form, but sees one's heart, i.e., one's inner state. (Ṣaḥīḥ Muslim, Hadith No. 2864-b)

Greenery Returned

In Delhi, there is a tree near my house. I call it a spiritual tree. I sit under it for hours on end for it gives me spiritual peace. Before the rainy season this tree was completely dried up. I thought that it had probably come to the end of its life. It was not going to be green and lush again, but after the rainy season, it started to become green again. Leaves began to appear on its branches and by the end of August, it had become completely green. Its freshness had returned completely.

This story is symbolic for human beings. It is necessary for a person's spiritual life to receive "water". One who lives without "water", will have a personality like a dried up tree.

For human life, divine inspiration is like life-giving water. Through it, one ought to establish an eternal spiritual bond with God. A bond of this kind will give one renewed freshness. If this bond is broken for any reason, he will become like a dried up tree.

Remembrance (dhikr) of God is the link to God Almighty. What does 'to remember God' mean? It is not just the repetition of certain words. It means to remember Him again and again in different situations. For example if you see a tree, you will see the miracle of God in it. You will exclaim, standing with your hand on your heart, "O God! The way you have made the tree green and fresh, so also in the same way make me like a green tree. I am just a dried up tree. You can turn me into a green tree by your inspiration." This experience does not relate to any one thing. It relates to all things. Everything in this world contains spiritual food. Wise is the one who is able to live in this world by taking spiritual food from everything.

The Price of Expected Acknowledgement

If a person were to be transported to the moon or if he found himself on some planet other than the earth, it would be a very shocking experience for him. He would see that, none of those things exist on the moon or on other planets which are necessary for a human being's survival. Look at the example of the fish out of water which wriggles about on dry land.

On the contrary, when a man takes stock of his life on earth, he finds that all those things are available here in abundance which are necessary for him to survive. For example, light, water, air, food, and the list is endless. Why is it that for human beings all the favourable conditions of life are already present on this earth? And does man understand the price of acknowledgement expected from him, for what has already been provided on the planet earth for him?

There are so many amazing phenomena in the universe. For instance the stars, the planets, the oceans, the mountains, etc. All these things are the creation of God. They all acknowledge God, but this is compulsory acknowledgement; it is not by choice.

Exceptionally, God has created man as a free creature. Man is required to acknowledge his God by his own choice. He should stand on the planet earth and say: "O God! I believe in Your existence without seeing You, and O God! I surrender myself before You without any compulsion. O God! I admit my helplessness in the face of Your power." That is the acknowledgement expected from a human being, on the basis of which all blessings have been bestowed in advance. Those who measure up to this acknowledgement will find that these blessings will continue to increase for them, but those who failed to acknowledge these blessings, will be deprived of them forever.

The Existence of God

Scientific studies of the universe have been regularly undertaken for almost five hundred years. Great minds have been engaged in this study. But how far has this scientific study taken us? This universe is so vast that it is beyond man's comprehension. According to the latest scientific research, man's knowledge barely encompasses 5% of universal realities. This 5% demonstrates the limitations of human knowledge. As one scientist has put it: "We are knowing more and more about less and less."

Knowing about God is to know about the Creator but experience tells us that so far, man's knowledge of God's creations is still infinitesimal. This being so, if anyone demanded exact information about the Creator, that would be totally an unscientific demand. Man has not yet been able to obtain complete knowledge about creation, how can he have complete knowledge about the Creator?

Creation exists within space and time, whereas the Creator exists beyond space and time. When man is so helpless that he cannot have knowledge of even those things which are within space and time, how can he bring under his observation the reality which exists beyond space and time? The reality is that, a person in this world can discover God only at the level of humility and not at the level of knowledge.

No Acknowledgement of God

Any normally generous father enjoys gifting things to his children. But let us see from what angle such gifts are regarded. Suppose he gives his son a car and then writes on the windshield "A Gift from Dad". This, in fact, is a case of ungratefulness. A blessing which is in actuality given by God, is thus attributed not to God but to a person. This is a case of a failure to acknowledge God's magnanimity and that is the greatest sin in this world.

The Qur'ān states that, when Prophet Sulaymān received a blessing he immediately said:

*hādhā min faḍli rabbī which means, "This is by the grace
of my Lord." (27:40)*

This is the only correct way to express true faith. That is, the Prophet described an apparently material blessing as "God's gift". True believers consider that everything belongs to God alone and acknowledge God by attributing everything to Him.

Whatever people get in this world is apparently by their own efforts. But this only appears to be so. The fact is that every single thing is a blessing from God. It is required of a person that he remove the veils in which reality is shrouded and by discovering the truth may say on receiving every blessing that this is God's gift given directly to me by God. Gratitude is the religious term for this acknowledgement. Only those who acknowledge God and are grateful to Him have a legitimate right to live in this world. On the contrary, those who fail to do so have no right to live in this world, for they are no better than sinners and intruders.

Animals in the Garb of Man

In February 2008, I went to an International Book Fair which was held in the Pragati Maidan in New Delhi. There were so many splendid book stalls on each side of the Pragati Maidan. And there was such a large number of people reading and buying books, that it appeared as if the Pragati Maidan had become a city of knowledge.

While I was walking inside the book fair, I noticed the strange sight of a dog, running around between the people. Apparently, it was also moving around like a human being but it did not know that there was a great deal of the world's knowledge in the form of these books. It had no desire to seek some light for itself from this vast world of knowledge.

The presence of this animal in the world of the book fair, reminded me of a verse of the Qur'ān which states that many people appear to be like human beings but are actually like animals. They only eat and drink in this world and then die. (47:12) God says in the Qur'ān:

God's signs are scattered everywhere in the present world. These signs introduce the Creator in the form of the creation. Those who discover God in this introduction and shape their lives accordingly, are not blind. But those who do not realize the presence of God are blind. They are like blind people in this world. That is why, in the end, they shall also be raised up in the state of blindness. Such people appear to be human but in reality they are like animals. This reality has remained hidden in this world, but in the end it will be revealed.

Discovery! Discovery! Discovery!

There is a maxim in Japan that you should discover new things everyday even if it be a method of putting thread in the needle. This saying is about material discoveries.

But this same principle applies equally in the case of realization and spirituality, although on a more elevated level. Spirituality is not something stagnant. It is a continuously growing entity like trees.

The fact is that the human mind is unlimited in its potential. The universe of facts external to the human mind are also boundless.This being so, one who keeps his mind in a state of continual awareness and reflects deeply upon things with full concentration at every moment, will continue to discover new realities everyday. For him the treasure trove of the discoveries will never come to an end.

Just as material food is sustenance for the body, similarly spiritual discoveries are food for realization. A constant supply of material food is a surety for the body's survival. Similarly, spiritual discoveries give life to God-realization and spirituality, and are a guarantee of human development.

Such discovery is an intellectual process. To continue this process uninterruptedly, two conditions are a must—reflection and saving one-self from distractions.

When these two conditions are met, the human being will definitely become a man of discovery. In consequence, nothing will stop him from making new discoveries.

Discovery is the spirit of life. Discovery is the source of intellectual development. Discovery makes a person complete. Without discovery a human being is just like a body without a spirit.

Patience, Introspection and the Willingness to Learn

After faith, three basic things are required in order to lead a meaningful life. They are patience, introspection and the willingness to learn lessons (tawassum). Without adopting these three things no one can become a true believer. After believing, every believer first of all faces the stage of finding out how to lead his life as a believer in his own environment. According to the law of nature, one finds unfavourable situations at every moment, which makes one intolerant. On all such occasions, a person has to remain patient, so that he may remain on the straight path without any deviation.

The second thing is introspection. In this testing ground, one makes mistakes again and again. It is essential that a person should hold himself accountable for these mistakes by subjecting himself to unbiased intro-spection. Without instant introspection the tendency to make mistakes will become an ineradicable part of one's personality. The third thing is the learning of lessons (tawassum). This means observing the phenom-ena of the universe in order to learn lessons from them, thus receiving spiritual nourishment from physical events. This is spiritual food for the seeker of truth, without which no one can become an aspirant to spiritual development. Religious life begins from faith. But it is only the starting point of spiritual life; it is not the final destination. After that man has to go through a course uninterruptedly, without completion of which no one can reach the stage of a true believer in the real sense. Basically, the components of this course are only three: patience, introspection and learning lessons. This course cannot be performed by any kind of formal rituals. This is entirely a conscious intellectual journey. Just by awakening one's consciousness, one can achieve success in this test.

God and Man

There was a dispute about a property between Mr. A and Mr. B. Mr. A said that a certain property belonged to him but that Mr. B had taken possession of it illegally. There were lengthy verbal interchanges between the two, but Mr. B was not ready to admit his mistake. Finally, Mr. A said to Mr. B that if he held God's book in his hand and said that this property was his, he would accept his claim and he could keep the property in his possession. Mr. B replied: "How does God come into the picture?"

In the present age, this is the case with almost everyone. Everyone does as he pleases, and when he is told to fear God, he asks, "How does God come into the picture?" This is sometimes said in words, and sometimes implied by people's action. This is true not just of the common men but also of the highly educated. For example, in present times, when advances have been made in the physical science and the laws of nature have been discovered, the modern educated class generally leave God out of their conception of the universe. They say, when all the events are happening according to the laws of nature, then why it is necessary to bring in God to explain the universe.

God is the Creator and Lord of this world. But it is strange that right throughout history, man has not given the importance to God which was His due. A person's very existence is a bounty conferred by God in the complete sense. Whatever he has in the form of wealth and children have all been bestowed upon him by God. Innumerable things like light, oxygen, food and water never cease to be available for man. The only one to give these things is God. But this greatest reality has been the least recognized in the whole of history. Man had only one thing to give to God and that was to acknowledge Him. But he has failed to do so.

Increased Faith

The Sun is 93,000,000 miles away from our earth and is 1,30,000 times bigger than it. The sun is not as solid as the earth, but is rather a big blaze of fire. Its temperature is 11,000 degrees Fahrenheit and is so hot that even the hardest of matter would melt on its surface. If the earth were to come closer to it, it would melt in less than one minute.

How does the sun shine and how does it give out such large amounts of heat and light? Since ancient times, until quite recently, it was believed that the sun was continuously burning like a wood or coal furnace. But when astronomical research revealed that it had been giving out light in this way for thousands of years this theory was proved wrong. Had there been any matter burning up inside the sun, it would have been extinguished long since, because nothing can go on burning for such a long time.

Now, the scientists have advanced the theory that the heat of the sun is the result of a process similar to that which takes place in the atomic bomb. The sun changes matter into energy. This is different from burning. Burning changes matter from one form to another. But when matter is changed into energy, very little matter is needed to produce a tremendous amount of energy. One ounce of matter is capable of producing enough energy to melt more than a million tons of rock.

In this universe, there are innumerable signs which show that a great Creator is at work behind its functioning. Without God Almighty, such a great creation could not have come into existence. The Qur'ān repeatedly exhorts the reader 'to reflect' on the signs of God spread out in the universe. This is a pure form of religious practice. It results in an extraordinary increase of faith in a believer.

The Spiritual Loss Caused by Greed

Greed is a person's greatest weakness: everyone feels that whatever he has is not enough. Everyone wants more and more. No one is satisfied with what he has. Psychology of this nature is destructive. The greatest loss it inflicts is that one is deprived of the blessings of special prayer to God. If an individual lives in a state of gratitude, that is, if he feels that whatever is required for leading his life in this world has been given to him by God, this will become a great point of reference for prayer.

These words will be uttered from the depths of his heart:

> *"O God, You have given me everything in the world."*
> *(14:34).*

Now I want the same in the world Hereafter as, You have promised in Your Book:

> *"Therein you shall have all that your souls desire, and*
> *therein you shall have all that you ask for." (41.31)*

A prayer said in gratitude is a high form of prayer. Such a prayer comes from one's heart with deep feelings. Such a prayer is the result of a prepared mind. Such a prayer represents one's entire existence.

In such prayer the choice of words is secondary. What is of prime importance is the internal feelings which stir up one's heart and mind. Such a prayer comes out of one's lips only when one comes so close to God that no distance remains between him and his Creator. In such a prayer words are just symbolic. The real, or actual du'ā' is that, which is heard only by the angels who then without delay deliver it to God.

Rational Knowledge and Inner Realization

There are two levels on which learning takes place. One is that of the acquisition of rational knowledge and the other is that of inner realization. Rational knowledge is only primary knowledge. Superior wisdom lies in the realization of truth at the level of inner insight. For instance, your awareness about your neighbour is based on rational knowledge. But what you know about your mother is at the level of conviction. Without using logic or reason and without the slightest doubt, you know that a certain woman is your mother. This is possible only at the level of total conviction.

This is true also of God, Who is the Creator and the Lord of man. Man's primary discovery about God takes place at the rational level. But such discovery ascends to a higher plane when man realizes without any doubt, through his inner perception, that God exists in the same way that he does. This is the case with the truths pertaining to God, for example, the truth that the Qur'ān is the word of God and the Prophet is God's Messenger. This knowledge is gained through rational thinking. But this is on the primary level of the realization of truth. The higher level of the realization of truth is the firm belief that man's inner perception becomes enough to accept these truths beyond any shadow of a doubt. There are two levels of knowledge in this matter: rational knowledge and divine knowledge. Rational knowledge is based on data, in comparison to which divine knowledge is that level of truth on which a person himself tries to reach this level of confidence on the basis of inner perception, where he does not need any data. His own inner feelings are the source of his conviction. It is that level of knowledge on which every individual has the conviction that a certain woman is his mother.

What is Islam?

The literal meaning of Islām is submission, that is, submission to God's will. Submission, in fact, is the name of that natural response from a person to God, the response that is expressed by human beings after their realization of God. It is with this submission that that life has developed which is called a religious life.

What is realization of God? The realization of God is the realization of that Being who has created man, who has granted man with a personality which is unique throughout the vast universe, Who has created the planet earth for man and who has established a unique arrangement for man's survival which is called the life support system.

A person's quest does not stop here but rather becomes a part of his life in the form of a process of discovery. Now, he discovers his relationship with God. He grasps the reality that he is not free but is under the command of God. In the process, he realizes that he is not free but has to act at God's behest and be accountable to Him. Death is not the end of his life, for another life begins after death, where he will stand before God, so that God may declare His final decision about his eternal future.

This process of discovery continues until he realizes that the end of his life is going to culminate in the form of either eternal Paradise or eternal Hell. This quest makes him extremely serious about the course his life should take. Now he plans his life anew. Now he redefines everything. If at first all his activities were self-oriented, now they are God-oriented. It is this very lifestyle which is called Islām.

One Serious Fallacy

People use reason extensively in their worldly matters. They think a lot and make thorough plans, but in the matter of religion they take a totally different path. Here, they think: let us go to some saint, ask him to pray for us, go to some dargāh, visit some elder or holy man, count out some words on the rosary, or do some rituals; and then they imagine they will have discharged their religious obligations. But this is applying double standards and is wholly insubstantial. One is not going to benefit from any of these courses of action in any way.

The truth is that, just as a person uses his reason in worldly matters so also shall he have to use his reason in matters of religion. He shall have to be entirely logical, without which no one can be a religious person in the real sense or be held deserving of Paradise.

The process of becoming a religious person in the full sense is a conscious act. For every man and woman, it is necessary to discover religion at a conscious level. A person should make his religiosity a conscious matter rather than just ritual obeisance. He should make his religion a fundamental part of his mind and heart. He should make his religious life a life of awareness just as he has made his worldly life a conscious experience. There is absolutely no exception to this rule. The greatest things that God has given a human being are his reason and his awareness. Those who do not find religion at this level and do not adopt religion in this sense will be held to be irreligious in the eyes of God, whether or not they are religious at the ritual level, that is whether or not they perform all the necessary rituals. Religiosity is a conscious act rather than the observance of a set of rituals.

Towards the Truth

Khālid ibn al-Walīd who was born in Makkah was initially an opponent of the Prophet of Islām and participated in several wars against him. Shortly before the conquest of Makkah (8 A.H), he came to Madinah and accepted Islām. While narrating the story of his acceptance of Islām, he said that before having accepted Islām, he had been engaged in activities against Islām, but he felt again and again that he was not at the right place, being the Prophet's rival. It weighed on his mind that he was not doing the right thing (al-Bidāyah wa'l-Nihāyah, vol. 4, p. 272).

This incident tells us of a psychological reality. God has created everyone with a particular nature, the nature desired by the Creator. As such, everyone who is not on the right path of God, at some point or the other, is overwhelmed by this feeling that the path he has taken is not his true path, that he was born for something else. This feeling is a warning given by nature. This feeling gives a person the opportunity to revise his stand and discover the right path for himself. But an individual is not always alerted by this warning and he continues to keep to the wrong path until he dies.

This feeling, in fact, is like a starting point in human life. This starting point gives a person the opportunity to set right the direction of his journey so that he may proceed towards the real destination. But the domination of desires, material interest, social biases and family pressures come in his path and he again goes back to the previous path, even after being warned by nature.

Everyone is engaged in such activities about which one's heart continuously tells him that he was not at the right place. There are many people who lead their lives in this state and die in the same state. Nevertheless, there are some who succeed in emerging from this intellectual morass and take to the right path demanded by their nature.

Modest Man

Self-centredness or a superiority complex is a natural syndrome which exists in everyone. This feeling brings about courage and confidence in a person. If a person has no ego, he will be deprived of self-confidence and in the absence of self-confidence no one can perform any great task. But it is necessary that one's feelings of self-confidence or superiority complex should be bound by limitations, that is, it should be reined in by the feeling of modesty. In the absence of such pressure, a person will lose his utility and his viability in social life. He will suffer from excessive pride (ahaṅkār). And without doubt there is nothing more destructive than excessive pride in this world.

There are two things in this world which make a person modest. One is a scientific bent of mind, the other, is his being God-fearing. A scientific bent of mind results from the realization of knowledge. And a God-fearing mind is the result of the realization of God.

When excessive pride builds up in a person, the reason is that he sees himself in relation to man, and since, there are many people he finds less excellent than himself, the feeling of ego or his own greatness begins to grow. But one who has a scientific bent of mind in the real sense, sees himself or his issues in relation to knowledge rather than in relation to the person who has knowledge. A person can be limited, but knowledge is unlimited. In relation to the person who has knowledge, one can think of oneself as greater than others but in relation to the vaster world of knowledge, everyone is lesser in stature. This feeling naturally produces modesty in a scientific or learned person.

Similarly one who has fear of God, or taqwā, will see his affairs in relation to God, the Almighty. Here too, the same principle applies with greater force. When one sees oneself in relation to creatures, one can rate oneself as being greater than others. But when one sees oneself in relation to God, everyone becomes small, in relation to God. No one is great. In this way the belief of a God-fearing man or woman makes him or her a balanced person.

The Final Explanation

Everything in this world is in its final state of perfection. The solar system is so complete that no other solar system can be conceived of. Our earth with its innumerable components is the final and perfect model. We cannot think of a better life support system than the one that exists in our world. Similarly, the mountains, the rivers, the trees, the animals and human beings, are all in their final state. Even the grass is perfect. No artist can make a better model of grass. The same is true of the creation plan. The creation plan is perfect. We cannot think of a better one.

God created a human being in the most superior form, then He placed him temporarily on our present earth and it was destined that in the eternal world after death, everyone would be punished or rewarded according to the deed he had performed in this world. This is the creation plan. For a creature like man, this is undoubtedly the best possible creation plan. No better creation plan can ever be conceived of.

For instance, every person has great desires. These desires are etched in his mind in the form of a beautiful concept of Paradise. Every man and woman wants to find a world where all desires are fulfilled without any obstacles. Every plan of life made by philosophers or thinkers, falls short of the fulfilment of human desires. The creation plan that comes before us in the form of the Hereafter is in its final form and has all the resources for or means of the fulfilment of desires. This aspect of the concept of the Hereafter is the final proof that it is the real concept of life. All other ideologies are mere suppositions.

The Spirit of Allāhu Akbar

The spirit of Islām in one phrase may be called the Allāhu Akbar spirit. The greatest prayer of Islām is ṣalāh, which is performed five times a day. There are, supererogatory (nāfil) prayers besides the regular prayers. In all these prayers, obligatory as well as voluntary, the expression Allāhu Akbar is repeated about three hundred times during the adhān (call to prayer) and prayer.

Allāhu Akbar means God is great. It is implicit in this that 'I am not great'. In this way, everyday all believers refresh their minds repeatedly with the idea that greatness pertains only to God: there is no greatness for them. Congregational prayer is a practical demonstration of this reality. In congregational prayer, all the believers make one person a prayer leader and the rest stand behind him. This is a social form of expression of the Allāhu Akbar spirit.

The purpose of saying Allāhu Akbar is to develop the spirit of modesty. When the spirit of modesty develops in a person in the real sense, it does not stop at any point: just as this spirit manifests itself before God during prayer, it manifests itself in like manner in relation to other human beings. The sign of the true believer is that the spirit of Allāhu Akbar, or the spirit of modesty, becomes a part and parcel of his everyday life.

Those who are imbued with this spirit of Allāhu Akbar will never display egoism or pride. They will never distance themselves from others on minor provocations. Working under others will appear to them as an act of worship. Their spirit will find happiness in surrender and modesty rather than in making others surrender to them. They will immediately accept their mistakes. They will be totally free from any desire for leadership.

The Tendency to Complain

On hearing an acquaintance complain about others, I pointed out that complaint is the killer of spirituality. Making complaints is such an evil that you must totally avoid doing so. He asked that how you could avoid complaining when there are so many reasons for complaint everyday in this world. I said this was how he was being put to the test and that in spite of complaints you yourself have to remain complaint-free in this world, in spite of negative experiences, you have to learn to live positively. This is a form of test paper for a person in this world. Everyone has to pass this test. One who passes this test is a successful person, and one who fails in this test has nothing left to hope for in this life. Furthermore this failure is eternal in nature, success is also everlasting.

The making of complaints is no simple matter. Complaints are always accompanied by ungratefulness. A heart full of complaints will have no feelings of gratitude. Furthermore, a complaint is like dirt. Even one speck of dirt defiles all of the water in the tub. In the same way, even a minor complaint deprives one of the feeling of gratefulness. A person ought to be so sensitive in this matter that he should never tolerate the erosion of gratitude. He should keep ignoring complaints, and keep ignoring those things which would cause him to complain, so that there is no dilution of his gratitude.

There is only one way to keep oneself away from this deadly evil and that is to nip it in the bud. Even if you have a minor complaint, you should reduce it to zero. Likewise, if there is one small thing to be thankful for you should magnify it so that it looks like something very great. This is the only strategy by which you can develop a personality in which there is no particle of ungratefulness. Those who live with the feeling of gratefulness have eternal Paradise in store for them.

The Greatest News of Today

The news vendor was calling out, "The greatest news of today!" "The greatest news of today!" I thought that the greatest news for the news vendor was that news which was printed on the front page of the newspaper. But the greatest news of today is actually what we see at the universal level.

What is this universal news? This universal news is that the sun which set yesterday has risen again today to give us light and heat, that the supply of oxygen in the air is continuing for us, the rotation of the earth is going on as precisely as it was going on yesterday, springs of fresh water are continuously flowing into the rivers, the air is flowing just as it was flowing yesterday, the earth remains firm and solid, the life support system which was there yesterday is still giving us succour today, all the usual activities of life are going on in our world, and so on.

In the morning, when you see the sun's rays entering in your room, it is not unusual that you get out of bed and call out aloud—another golden morning! This is true not only for the sunrises, it is rather true for every event of nature, for even those events which appear small are intrinsically as great as other more spectacular events.

Discovering this extraordinary aspect of an ordinary event is, in a sense, the learning of a lesson (15:75) and it is this learning of lessons from the signs of nature that is the biggest source of the realization of God.

Such realization is a living experience. It is another name for continuous discovery. It means finding spiritual food in the material world. There is nothing mysterious about it. Realization of God is the equivalent of intellectual development.

The Voice of the Universe

A radio set is placed on your table. Apparently, it is not working for there is no sound coming from it. But when you switch it on, all of a sudden you hear sounds or voices, meaningful voices uttering words which are understandable. Afterwards, when you switched off the radio set, all of a sudden all broadcasting ceased. Now the speaking radio had fallen silent. It was still the same radio set placed on your table but it was not emitting any audible sounds.

The universe is also a huge divine radio set, broadcasting its messages at all times. At every moment, it is relaying voices. Every day and night, morning and evening it is announcing what the nature of this world is; why a human being has been born into this world; wherein one's success and failure lie; whence one has come and whither one will return; what the divine criterion is of the truth and falsehood by which one will be judged after death and according to which his or her eternal future will be decided.

This happens just as we hear the voices of the man-made radio when we switch it on and also keep our ears open. But the voices emanating from the greater radio of the universe can be heard only by those who open their minds and are attentive to it. The universal radio is apparently broadcasting its message in silent language, but those who are serious about wanting to hear it, find this far more audible than other voices. It is scattered throughout the vastness of the heavens, it is as clear as the light of the sun, it is apparent in the waves of the rivers and the oceans, it enters into us in the form of air. In short, right from the plants of the earth to the stars of the heavens, there is nothing which is not engaged in communicating this universal message—the true listener is the one who listens to this universal voice and seeks guidance for his life from it.

The Example of a Tree

The tree is a divine enterprise. The tree begins with a small seed within which all the potential exists for it to produce a trunk, roots, branches, twigs and leaves. It just has to find a favourable environment in which to start growing. If you sow the seed under a stone, you cannot expect the desired result. But when the seed is sown in soil, it is as if, the soil becomes soft and helps in letting it take root, and all of a sudden, the seed is linked with the entire universe. In a way, it is as if the whole universe had been created for its nurture.

Many factors come together to provide the seed with food. The layers of soil contain minerals and salts which, when dissolved by rainwater, are assimilated by the roots, which in turn supply them to the rest of the plant and then the tree starts growing. Right from the earth to the sun, the entire mechanism of the universe becomes activated to produce the different weather conditions which will bring the heat and cold and rain necessary for the plant to grow into a full grown tree.

This tree so harmoniously becomes a part of the entire universe that it does not clash with anything else in its environment. If it takes water from the ground, it also gives out moisture through its leaves and con- tributes to the formation of rain clouds. If the tree takes food from the ground, it produces leaves and flowers, then it lets its leaves and flowers fall on the ground in order to fertilize the soil. If it takes carbon diox- ide from the air, it returns to its surroundings another more beneficial element in the form of oxygen. Although separate from the universe, it relates to the entire universe in such a manner that it does not clash with anything else.

The tree, moreover, presents a beautiful picture to the human eye and gives off a lovely fragrance to the passerby. For those who want food it has delicious fruits to offer. It may also be cut down for those who need wood. The tree meets many needs and is guaranteed to fulfil human expectations for all time to come.

Half of the tree is above the ground and half of it is below the ground. The tree, moreover, is so deep-rooted that it needs no support and its roots are so firmly entrenched in the soil that no one can uproot it. It rises so high in its surroundings that it is always able to have sunlight.

The Qur'ān has likened the believer to a tree. This shows what qualities the believer should have. In the believer all those qualities exist at the human level which exist at the material level in the tree. A believer has to consciously do of his own free will what the tree is doing while governed by nature. The believer, of his own free will, has to create a green world which the tree brings about as a matter of compulsion as it has no freedom. A tree has to follow the laws of nature.

The tree is a growing phenomenon and, similarly, a believer too is a growing phenomenon. The believer is a human being who, because of his divine thinking, is able to make the entire universe spiritual food for his realization of God.

REMEMBRANCE OF GOD

What is Remembrance?

Mawlānā ʿAbd al-Majīd Daryābādī (d. 1977) interpreted this verse of the Qurʾān (2:152) "So remember Me, I will remember you," as follows:

> *"Abū Bakr Jassās al-Rāzī (d. 370) took the meaning of "remembrance" as signs of God and thinking about God's majesty and power. And he regarded this form of worship as superior to other types of remembrance (such as saying God's name while counting the beads on the rosary)."* (Aḥkām al-Qurʾān, vol. 1, p. 114)

The fact is that we understand the being of God only through those phenomena or attributes of God which are scattered everywhere in our own existence and across the universe. We achieve the realization and discovery of God through contemplation on these phenomena of nature.

The reality is that, remembrance does not mean verbal repetition of God's name. Remembrance means contemplation on God's creation to discover God's greatness through the wisdom and perfection of His works. This is remembrance, and through it, one can achieve a higher level of realization of God.

It is a fact that we cannot observe God's Being, yet, we can definitely see glimpses of God in His creation. This contemplation on God's creation is another name for remembrance of God, and through it one is able to achieve that high level of firm faith which is called realization of God.

Trying to observe God's Being leads one either to ecstasy or to confusion, and both of these are actually undesirable. In this case, the most desirable thing is divine realization, which is achieved through contemplation and deep thinking. There is no other way to reach this goal.

Remembrance of God

The Qur'ān states

"Remembrance of God is surely the greatest thing."
(29:45)

In other words, it means that, for a person, remembrance of God is the greatest form of worship.

This remembrance of God is what is most desired of a human being. Therefore, the Qur'ān adjures us to remember God very frequently (33:41).

What is meant by remembrance of God? It does not mean any numerical or statistical exercise but rather it is one's mental condition. According to a tradition, 'Ā'ishah, the Prophet's wife, said: "The Prophet Muḥammad used to remember God on every occasion." (Ṣaḥīḥ Muslim, Hadith No. 373) One can understand the meaning of remembrance of God from this tradition.

Abundantly remembering God means that whatever a person sees or whatever he experiences, he should make it a point of reference for the remembrance of God.

Everything should remind him of God. Every experience should become a reason for strengthening his faith. Every study and observation should bring him nearer to God.

Point of Reference for Prayer

In chapter 4 of the Qur'ān, there is a verse about the law of inheritance which is as follows:

> *"If other relatives, orphans or needy people are present at*
> *the time of the division, then provide for them out of it,*
> *and speak kindly to them." (4:8)*

It means that, at the time of the division of a legacy, if certain family members are present who do not have a share, provide for them out of it. Do not send them away empty-handed. Apparently this is a verse about inheritance, but there is an important point of reference in it for prayer. When a believer reads this verse, he will be so moved that, he will say:

"O God! This is my case in relation to Paradise. I have not done such deeds as make me worthy of Paradise. But in this verse of the Qur'ān You have set forth the principle that if some people come at the time of division and are not entitled to get a share in accordance with the law, even then, out of compassion some things should be given to them out of the goods of inheritance."

In this verse of the Qur'ān there is great solace for a believer. A person can say in connection with this verse: "O God! I am an entirely undeserving person. But this Quranic verse tells us that Your mercy is so vast that it also reaches out to the unworthy. O God! Your mercy is a ray of hope for me. Referring to Your own principle, I would ask that despite of my being undeserving, You let me share in Your mercy. You can give a place in Paradise even to an undeserving candidate such as me, although Paradise has been created just for deserving candidates. I admit that, according to the Sharī'ah law, I do not deserve Paradise, but according to the law of Mercy, please grant me a place in Your Paradise."

Helplessness and Power

In chapter 35 of the Qur'ān there is a verse which says:

> "O men! It is you who stand in need of God—God is self-sufficient, and praiseworthy." (35:15)

The same thing is mentioned in a ḥadīth:

> "O my servants! All of you have strayed, except for those whom I will show the way. You ask Me for guidance, I will guide you. O my servants, you are all hungry, except those whom I feed. You ask me for food, I will give you food." (Ṣaḥīḥ Muslim, Hadith No. 2577)

God certainly gave a human being a perfect existence, but he does not have any personal choice. Human beings are completely helpless creatures. This helplessness is compensated for by God in this world. This helplessness is compensated for only according to need. This has been mentioned thus in the Qur'ān:

> "He has given you all that you asked of Him." (14:34)

In Paradise in the Hereafter, this helplessness will be compensated for according to one's desire:

> "Therein you shall have all that your souls desire." (41:31)

The discovery of this truth is the greatest realization, discovering one's total helplessness in comparison to the Omnipotence of God Almighty is the beginning of realization of truth. The door of realization does not open to any person without this discovery. Paradise is for the realized soul, not for the unrealized soul.

Divine Prayer

The Qur'ān tells the story of how Ādam made the mistake of eating the fruit of the forbidden tree, and was suddenly deprived of God's mercy. He subsequently, felt very perturbed and prayed to God for forgiveness. In the words of the Qur'ān:

*"Then Ādam received some words [of prayer] from his
Lord and He accepted his repentance. He is the Forgiving
one, the Merciful." (2:37)*

The word talaqqā used in this verse, literally means 'to receive'. It
means that Ādam received some words from his Lord, then accordingly,
he prayed to God, and then God accepted his supplication. Here, the
question arises as to what the form of this talaqqā was. It does not mean
that God called to Ādam, or that an angel came and inculcated in him
these words. It would not be correct to make such an assumption here.

The fact is that it was a matter of inspiration. There is a ḥadīth to this
effect:

*"This is a light which is put in the heart of the believer."
(Muṣannaf Ibn Abī Shaybah, Hadith No. 34315)*

When an intense feeling of having erred builds up in a person, he turns
towards God with grief and repentance and in total surrender to his
Creator. At that time, he experiences spiritual feelings at the psychological level. This feeling becomes converted into certain particular words.
This is called rabbānī prayer. This kind of divine prayer is advance news
of the acceptance of prayer itself.

Who will receive the blessings of this kind of divine prayer?

Only one graced with such prayer as can bring himself on to a level of
total servitude, who can discover the full reality of the fact that he is the
taker and God is the giver. When such feelings are experienced by a person, they give rise to moments when he establishes a special relationship
with God. At that time divine words of supplication and remembrance
of God start pouring out of his lips. The name of such inspired divine
words of prayer is rabbānī prayer.

Gratefulness in the State of Ungratefulness

The Qur'ān tells the story of Ādam and Iblīs in detail. It explains how
Iblīs was deprived of God's blessings because of his refusal to bow to

Ādam. At that time Iblīs said to God:

> *"Because you have put me in the wrong, I will lie in ambush for them on Your straight path: then I will surely come upon them from before them and from behind them and from their right and from their left, and then You will find most of them ungrateful." (7:16–17)*

In this verse, his being put in the wrong implies his being put to the test. What Iblīs wanted to say was that under normal conditions, he was able to follow divine commands but the command of bowing to Ādam was too hard a test for him to pass and, as a result he was distanced from God's mercy. Then he expressed his intention of doing the same to all human beings until the majority failed in the test and took to the path of ungratefulness.

We learn from the Qur'ān that Iblīs has no power over man (15:42). Then the question arises as to how he will make man ungrateful.

Actually, there are always reasons for being ungrateful in the life of this world. To lead a life of gratefulness it is necessary to learn the art of being grateful, even where there are reasons for ungratefulness.

This is the point where Iblīs finds an opportunity to mislead man into becoming an ungrateful servant of God. As a result, he fails to turn ingratitude into gratitude. Every incident of ungratefulness is made a pretext for becoming ungrateful, and finally a person is forever deprived of whatever blessings gratefulness would bring him.

Remembrance is a Thinking Process

Of the admonitions given in the language of commands in the Qur'ān, one is of that for which the expression 'remembrance of God' has been used. This command appears in several verses of the Qur'ān. One of the verses exhorts believers to "remember God often." (33:41)

Remembering (dhikr) is a meaningful reality, not just a turn of phrase. It is a fact though that when a person remembers someone, he remembers him first by words. For instance, when Zaid has to be remembered, the word Zaid will first come to mind. But in terms of memory, the position of the word is not real but relative. Just as when you remember Zaid, a man will come to your mind, when you remember God, the Lord of the worlds, He will naturally come to your mind as the Owner and Lord of the universe; One whose blessings are so many that they cannot be counted. Contemplation or deep thinking is automatically involved in remembering.

A tradition has been mentioned in different books of ḥadīth. ʿĀ'ishah said:

> *"The Prophet Muḥammad used to remember God on
> every occasion." (Ṣaḥīḥ Muslim, Hadith No. 373)*

According to this tradition, frequent remembrance of God means that every experience and observation should create God-oriented thinking to the point where the whole world of nature will become a reminder of God for a person. Remembrance is not just the repetition of some words. The natural way of remembrance is the awakening of man's mind to such an extent that throughout the different circumstances of his life, he begins to experience God in everything. Everything becomes a means of reminding him of God.

Sincere Repentance

Chapter 66 of the Qur'ān, tells us what sincere repentance (tawbah) is. Verse 8 says:

> *"Believers, turn to God in sincere repentance. Your Lord
> may well forgive your bad deeds and admit you into gar-
> dens watered by running streams, on a Day when God
> will not abase the Prophet and those who have believed
> with him. Their light will shine out ahead of them and*

on their right, and they will say: 'Lord perfect our light for
us, and forgive us; You have power over all things.'" (66:8)

Sincere repentance means pure repentance or true repentance. The commentator al-Qurṭubī wrote that, scholars have given the word "repentance" twenty three meanings. (Tafsīr al-Qurṭubī, vol. 18, p. 197) But the fact is that it does not have 23 different meanings, it has rather different aspects of pure repentance. These aspects are not limited to just 23. They number more than that.

If a person commits a sin, he later realizes his mistake. He must sincerely repent in his heart and if he returns to God with strong commitment, this is called pure repentance.

If the person truly repents, his whole life will change. At first, if his way of thinking was ungodly, now his thinking will be godly. If he was not sincere earlier, now he will become sincere. If at first he led an irresponsible life, he will now start to live a responsible life. If at first he misused his freedom he will now be strictly bound by divine principles. Earlier, if he had no fear of the Hereafter, he will now start living in the fear of the Hereafter. Repentance changes a human being and such repentance is called true repentance.

The Importance of Gratitude

The very first verse of the Qur'ān reads:

"All praise is due to God, the Lord of the Universe." (1:2)

This verse shows the importance of gratitude. The truth is that of all the acts of Islām, gratitude is the only act which a person can perform in its highest ideal form. But for various reasons in other spheres such as worship, ethics, social dealings, and so on, man's performance falls short of the ideal. The performance of the 'worship' of gratitude relates, however, to the heart and mind, and as such, it is possible for a person to perform it in its ideal form. In gratitude, he can offer all his best feelings, all his best thoughts to God. Such perfection can be expressed solely as a matter of gratitude.

What is gratitude? Gratitude is, in fact, another name for acknowledgement. What is called acknowledgement in human matters is called gratefulness in the matter of God. It is essential for every person to awaken his or her consciousness to such a high level that everything he or she possesses should be seen as God's gift in the full sense. One may then in total gratitude utter the words: "Praise be to God." With full consciousness of God's blessings and mercy, one may utter the words: "Praise be to God, Lord of the worlds."

This is true thanksgiving and there is no doubt about it that thanksgiving is the noblest form of worship.

In the present world, what is called life support system exists on a large scale. Here everything is created in such a way that in the total sense, it is favourable to a human being. The whole world is a custom-made world. Given this situation, when a person is free to live in this world, and utilize its resources, he should be filled with feelings of gratefulness and acknowledgement: a person, it should be borne in mind, has received all the precious things of this world free of cost.

True thankfulness is the price we have to pay for all these things. Those who do not pay this price are like usurpers in this world. Living in this world without this feeling of gratefulness is an unpardonable sin, for both men and women.

The Extended Meaning of the Qur'ān

The Qur'ān is a universal book. Its message is an eternal one. As well as having a primary meaning, the verses of the Qur'ān have an extended meaning. To understand this deeper meaning of the Qur'ān, it is very important to understand this fact.

For example, there is a verse in the Qur'ān about the dawn prayer (ṣalāt al-fajr): "... the recitation at dawn is indeed witnessed." (17:78) This means that the time of the dawn prayer is a time of tranquillity and solitude.

That is why the recitation at dawn is given special mention.

This verse can have the extended meaning that the believer should say the morning prayer at the appointed time, and then go to a park to walk, or go to a place where there is greenery of nature. In the morning there is an angelic environment at such a place. In such an environment, a person should look at the signs of God. He should recite the verses of the Qur'ān. He has to discover God in His creation. One scenario is that after saying the morning prayer, people should go to such a place together where they remember God collectively in that natural environment and talk about God. They remember the perfection of God in scenes of nature. They endeavour to get spiritual food for themselves in an atmosphere of spirituality. This is remembrance at dawn, which is an extended form of recitation of the Qur'ān at the ṣalāt al-fajr prayer. Such a course of action is actually a way to increase faith, whether individually or collectively.

This is true of each verse of the Qur'ān. One meaning of a verse of the Qur'ān is that which is known through its particular cause of revelation (sabab al-nuzūl). This is the initial or primary meaning of the verse. In addition to this, each verse of the Qur'ān has an extended meaning.

By taking into account these extended meanings it will be possible for the faithful to keep discovering new meanings in the Qur'ān.

The Book of Recitation or The Book of Obedience

There was a property dispute between Mr. A and Mr. B, both of whom were Muslims. Both claimed ownership of a particular piece of property. Mr. A said to Mr. B: "If you take the Qur'ān in hand and say that this property is mine, then I will withdraw my claim and accept your right to the property." Mr. B asked, "What is the connection between the Qur'ān and this issue?"

If Mr. B was a Muslim, why did he ask such a question? The reason is that the present day Muslims have given up the book of God. They have shown their disregard for it, as mentioned in the Qur'ān (25:30). The truth is that, for present-day Muslims, the Qur'ān has become a book of recitation and not a book of guidance or obedience. This mindset has become common in Muslims today. The above-mentioned event is an example of that very mindset. I asked many people who were running institutions and movements in the name of Islām, whether they had read the Qur'ān again and again before starting their work to ascertain what work, according to the Qur'ān, they should be doing. But hardly anyone answered in the affirmative. There will be some people who will read commentaries of the Qur'ān, or who will try to learn the Arabic language, so that they may understand the Qur'ān directly. But such individuals will be hard to find, who have made the Qur'ān a guide book for their words and deeds. This is the greatest negligence on the part of the present-day Muslims. Not until Muslims make the Qur'ān their personal guide book, will their affairs be set properly in order.

The Importance of the Study of the Qur'ān

'Abd Allāh ibn 'Abbās, a senior Companion of the Prophet, once observed that one who recited the Qur'ān would never become decrepit in his old age. (Mustadrak al-Ḥākim, Athar No. 3952) Here, reciting the Qur'ān means making a study of the Qur'ān. One who makes a thorough study of the Qur'ān will continue deriving intellectual food from it, and in this way he will continue to have his energy boosted. As a result, he will not become decrepit in his old age. His mind will forever be active. His body may age but his mind will not. Research tells us that there is a difference between mind and body. Purely physiologically, our body grows old, but our brain does not. If one saves oneself from negative thinking and becomes a positive thinker in the full sense, his mind will never age. Anyone making a thorough study of the Qur'ān will continue to receive intellectual food for creative thinking from the Qur'ān on a daily basis. He will never suffer from intellectual starvation. His mind will always be active and full of creativity.

Just as material food gives energy to the body, in a similar way intellectual discoveries also are sources of energy. The most thrilling experience for a person is the experience of discovery. Those who study the Qur'ān in depth continually have such experiences. It is this creative experience which acts as a deterrent to the brain becoming old and ineffective in old age.

The Morning Recitation of the Qur'ān

The Qur'ān says that the recitation of the Qur'ān at the dawn prayer (ṣalāt al-fajr) "is indeed witnessed." (17:78) "Witnessed" here means validated by the angels.

We learn from a tradition that the early morning is a time especially favourable to God-realization, when in peace and solitude the angels in great numbers become witnesses to the recitation of the believer. There is nothing mysterious about this. It is the special task of the angels to engender spiritual feelings within a person and the peaceful time of the morning is propitious for this angelic action.

There is another dimension to this. For instance, you say your dawn (fajr) prayer at the prayer time and hear the long recitation of the Qur'ān from the lips of the imām. Afterwards, moved by the recitation of the Qur'ān, you leave the mosque and go to some open place where in the environment of nature, with all its greenery, you reflect upon nature, then you feel that your Quranic thinking and the external environment have become one. In silent language the scenes of nature bear witness to your Quranic thinking being indeed a universal reality, and that the universe is also functioning on the same pattern.

When, in the morning, a person reflects upon the messages of God in the peaceful environment of nature, he starts feeling the presence of God. Then he has that state induced in him which has been thus expressed in an injunction in a ḥadīth:

"Worship God as if you are seeing Him." (Ṣaḥīḥ al-Bukhārī, Hadith No. 50)

This state cannot be arrived at on one's own. It is produced undoubtedly with the help of the angels. This is to testify to inner thinking of the believer. This is a superior form of worship. And such an experience is not possible without the support of the angels.

Pondering over the Qurʾān

Chapter 38 of the Qurʾān tells us the purpose of the revelation of the Qurʾān:

"This is a blessed book which we sent down to you (Muḥammad) for people to ponder over its messages, and for those with understanding to take heed." (38:29)

Pondering does not just mean recitation of the Qurʾān and understand its meaning. This method is also without doubt beneficial, but to reach the higher meaning of the Qurʾān in this way is not sufficient.

There are two basic aspects of pondering upon the Qurʾān—contemplation and duʿāʾ (supplication). What is contemplation? I came to understand it from one particular incident. A Muslim writer with whom I often spent some time used to say, "I am a lover of Ghalib." Ghalib was a great 19th century Urdu poet, and my acquaintance went on to explain the deeper meaning of the couplets of Ghalib. He said that he not only read the poems of Ghalib, but rather lived in them. As he put it, "The couplets of Ghalib are always in my mind. I am always thinking about them."

This is the real meaning of pondering. It does not just mean trying to understand the meaning of the Qurʾān while reciting it. It means that it should dominate your thinking. The verses of the Qurʾān should stay in your conscious mind at all times. You have to sleep with the Quranic verses and wake up with them. Pondering upon the Qurʾān is the development of an intellectual relationship with the divine revelation.

The second necessary condition is that one should keep praying to God. Prayer (du'ā') does not just mean that one should keep repeating such words as:

> *"O My Lord increase me in knowledge." (The Qur'ān, 20:114)*

Prayer begins with the discovery of one's helplessness. A person who cannot recognize his helplessness in this way is not properly equipped to do du'ā' or supplication to God.

Stirring Up of a Revolution in the Human Personality

The Qur'ān has this to say about its recitation:

> *"True believers are those whose hearts tremble with awe at the mention of God, and whose faith grows stronger as they listen to His revelations. They are those who put their trust in their Lord." (8:2)*

At another place the Qur'ān has this to say:

> *"When they listen to what has been sent down to the Messenger, you see their eyes overflowing with tears, because of the Truth they recognize. They say, 'Our Lord we believe, so count us among those who bear witness.'" (5:83)*

The Qur'ān directly conveys God's words. It has divine majesty. It intensifies feelings of servitude. It has that divine light which, if it goes within one, brightens up one's entire inner existence. It has that light of truth which, when it enters the heart, it can cause it to fall to pieces, just as Mount Ṭūr fell to pieces where God's light fell upon it. Recitation of the Qur'ān is not just the mouthing of words. Its impact is such that both the heart and the mind are set on fire. This is why, reciting the Qur'ān again and again is a means of stirring up a revolution in the human personality.

The recitation of the Qur'ān is not like the recitation of books in any simple sense. It is the study of the word of God. It is as if indirectly entering into conversation with God. This being so, the recitation of the Qur'ān should induce that state of which it is deserving. If this state is not aroused within one by these extraordinary Words of God, it will mean that he has not given due attention to the recitation of the Qur'ān. He has been negligent. He has not recited the Qur'ān with keen awareness.

While reciting the Qur'ān a person should have within him a feeling of awe before God. He should feel that he has come near to God. Reciting the Qur'ān should become like a living introduction to God. On the one hand, he finds servitude in recitation and, on the other hand, he finds the Glory and Majesty of God.

Pondering on the Qur'ān

Chapter 38 of the Qur'ān tells us:

> *"This is a blessed Book which We sent down to you (Muḥammad), for people to ponder over its messages, and for those with understanding to take heed." (38:29)*

Pondering, in this verse, means deep thinking. Such thinking in actual fact is a special way of using one's mind. This means that the Qur'ān has to be read with an open mind, for one can find intellectual food through contemplation rather than by mere recitation.

The right method of studying the Qur'ān is to read the Qur'ān by using one's mind and not just by recitation. Similarly, when one reads a portion of the Qur'ān in prayer one should do so with an open mind.

When a person reads the Qur'ān in this way, it will repeatedly happen that he will be struck by some word or verse of the Qur'ān. On such occasions, he should pause and reflect on this. In this way, he will receive intellectual food from the Qur'ān.

For instance, when you read the Qur'ān, you will come across this verse:

> *"And for their words God will reward them with Gardens*

through which rivers flow, wherein they shall abide forever. That is the reward of those who do good." (5:85)

When you read this verse you will be reminded of this ḥadīth:

"Whoever said there is no god but God will enter heaven."
(Musnad al-Bazzār, Hadith No. 10080)

This will make you think about what the relation is between the two. Then, upon reflection, this point will become clear to you that the "words" mentioned in the ḥadīth have been explained in the Qur'ān. That is, the "words" for which one has been promised Paradise, means words of deep realization of the truth and not just the utterance of a particular word. This is called contemplation.

The Verse of God's Throne

There is a verse in chapter 2 of the Qur'ān, commonly called the verse of God's throne, or Āyat al-Kursī, which states:

"God: there is no deity save Him, the Living, the Eternal one. Neither slumber nor sleep overtakes Him. To Him belong whatsoever is in the heavens and whatsoever is on the earth. Who can intercede with Him except by His permission? He knows all that is before them and all that is behind them. They can grasp only that part of His knowledge which He wills. His throne extends over the heavens and the earth; and their upholding does not weary Him. He is the Sublime, the Almighty One!" (2:255)

Some statements are axiomatic, that is, they are self-evident truths. They need no further explanation or reasoning to uphold them. For example, there is a mathematical principle that if two lines are parallel they can never meet. This needs no proof. While parallel lines are examples of entities in the material world which are measurable and can be reasoned about, there are immeasurable, intangible things in the spiritual world which are palpably true and need no further explanation. The attributes and powers of God as are given above in the Āyat al-Kursī are just such examples. The statement made in this verse needs no additions of details. To subject them to any such interpretation would be to lessen their strength and diminish their glory.

First Favour, Second Favour

Addressing the Prophet Mūsā, God says:

> *"Indeed, We showed Our favour to you before also."*
> *(Qur'ān: 20:37)*

The background of this verse is that the Prophet Mūsā was born into an Israelite family in ancient Egypt. Pharaoh, the king in those days, wanted to exterminate the Israelites and, to this end, had ordered the killing of any male child born into an Israelite home. Mūsā would have met the same fate, if God had not saved him by divine intervention.

This was God's first favour to Mūsā. Later when Mūsā was granted prophethood, and he asked God to give him Hārūn as his helper, God answered his prayer as an exceptional gift for Mūsā. This meant that, at his request, God had assigned another Prophet to help him. These favours are recorded in the Qur'ān. The first was that of God saving Mūsā from being killed in childhood. And the second favour was, at his request, an ordinary person being made a Prophet for his support. One aspect of the Qur'ān is that there is a primary application of its verses and along with it there is the secondary application. This incident of the Prophet Mūsā is also of the kind where, in everyone's life, some special event takes place in which one is saved from being harmed by the special succour of God. A person has to discover this first favour of God to him, so that with that reference he may request for a second favour from God.

> *"We showed Our favour to you before also"* alludes to this.

If an individual is able to discover the first favour, then there will be a deep feeling engendered within him and with reference to the first favour, he will be able to request God for the second favour. This is a great point of reference for human beings which is found in the lives of all men and women, provided, they are able, on deep reflection to discover this reference.

There was once an individual who suffered great harm from some accident in his youth, and he became very depressed. Finally he decided to commit suicide. God helped him in time and he was saved from committing suicide. In his later years, after much study, or when he came to know of the realities of life, he remembered that incident in his youth and in his prayers to God he said that had he killed himself by committing suicide, today he would have found himself in the fire of Hell: "It was by Your favour that I was saved for the first time from Hell fire. After death, again I shall have to face the same situation. Then I request You to save me from Hell fire once again. You did me this favour the first time. Now you can do the same favour a second time and complete Your blessing upon me."

The most effective prayer is one which is made with some point of reference. Some point of reference is always there in everyone's life which renders the prayer very effective. But usually people do not give any thought to this and that is why they remain deprived of this precious reference. Due to this unawareness they only know the minimal form of prayer. And in the name of prayers, they learn some words by rote and keep repeating them.

This is without doubt a great deprivation. When a person knows a superior form of prayer and yet he keeps repeating this inferior form of prayer, that is a greater deprivation than anything else.

Learning the words of prayer by rote is without doubt a diminution of prayer. The superior form of prayer is to ask for another blessing with reference to a previous blessing.

Convert Loss into Gain

Chapter 12 of the Qur'ān tells the story of Prophet Yūsuf and how because of the misdeeds of his step brothers, his father, Prophet Ya'qūb, was deprived of his two beloved sons. At the time of this incident, he uttered this prayer:

> *"I only complain of my anguish and my sorrow to God."*
> *(12:86)*

These words of Prophet Yaʿqūb tell us an important truth: that when the believer faces any difficult situation or experiences anguish, he does not fall to complaining like an ordinary person, but rather, mindful of his faith, turns his grief into prayer. He bows down to God and prays to Him to change his loss into gain.

When someone faces the experience of grief and loss, there are two ways in which he can react. One is to look at the relevant human element in his affliction and the other is to turn to God. Those who only look at the human aspect of things, never cease to complain about human beings. But one who starts remembering God after an untoward experience he will make the Giver his central focus instead of the one who has caused him to suffer. His mind will become hopeful instead of remaining plunged in despair. Prayer has the greatest power to be of support to the believer in difficult times. Prayer is the source of this trust that no loss is final in this world: in every loss there is hidden gain.

There are moments in every person's life when he feels helpless. At such moments, prayer to God brings a person comfort and peace. For any individual, prayer is the best source of crisis management.

Discovery of Total Absence of One's Power

Chapter 90 of the Qur'ān has this to say:

> *"We have created man into a life of toil and trial. Does*
> *he think then that no one has power over him?" (90:4–5)*

Here "man" denotes the whole human race. And toil (kabad) means suffering. In this verse "power" has been mentioned along with kabad (suffering). This tells us about the reason for suffering. God created man with extraordinary capacity. But along with that he was placed in such circumstances as were always fraught with some problem, such as suffering.

Even those who have got everything they have ever striven for are not free from suffering. This has been done so that a person may discover his total lack of power. Although apparently a human being seems to have power, he still has his share of suffering. Suffering is a timely reminder of God's absolute power.

Looked at from this point of view, suffering is, in fact, a blessing in disguise. God, in spite of being the greatest reality, remains unseen. By means of compulsory suffering, God wants a person to experience His presence.

Wahb ibn Munabbih (d. 110 AH) once observed:

> *"Suffering comes so that man may pray from his heart."*
> *(Al-Shukr, Ibn Abī al-Dunyā, Athar No. 133)*

This does not refer to just the words of prayer. This means that a person's mind is awakened and noble feelings are engendered within him. He starts discovering God's attributes in different forms. And when this happens, he utters such words of prayer as befit extraordinary circumstances.

Constant Complaining

The Qur'ān describes how Satan became angry when God asked him to bow to Ādam. He said to God that if he were given the chance, he would cause Ādam's whole race to go astray. At the time of throwing down this challenge, he said,

> *"Most of them You will not find grateful." (7:17)*

There are countless blessings given by God to human beings. Yet man, instead of acknowledging these blessings, becomes ungrateful. The reason for this lies in the character of Satan, or Iblīs, who was a jinn (18:50). God heaped countless blessings on the jinn, who were invisible. He gave them existence, freedom of choice, and extraordinary options. He gave them a long life. For their survival in this world, God provided them with every necessity. Despite this, why was Iblīs so ungrateful to God? The reason was that he was so full of resentment that he forgot all of God's blessings. Instead, he fell to constant complaining. He exaggerated his grudges so much that he could not think of anything but complaining.

In his uniquely evil way, Satan warps human nature in such a manner that, human beings come to make every event a matter of complaint and ignore all other good things. He so overemphasizes the negative side of things that all the other positive aspects of things would simply disappear. In spite of having all the objects deserving of gratitude, the individual becomes ungrateful. Those who find themselves beset by such state of feelings should understand that they are being influenced by Satan. Such people should introspect and immediately repent, otherwise they will suffer the chastisement of God.

The Increase in Blessings

The Qur'ān states:

> *"And remember also the time when your Lord declared: if you are grateful, I will surely bestow more favours on you; but if you are ungrateful, then know that My punishment is severe indeed." (14:7)*

In this verse of the Qur'ān, the increase in blessings (more favours) applies to one who, grateful for the blessings of God in this world, will receive his reward in the form of Paradise in the Hereafter. Actually, gratitude is the other name for acknowledgement. Acknowledgement of blessing on receiving a reward is the greatest form of worship. And this worship is something which will make a person worthy of Paradise.

What is meant by blessing? Blessing, actually, is the sense of enjoyment. If something can give us joy, it is because we have the sense of enjoyment. Where there is no sense of enjoyment, nothing can be a source of pleasure.

Human beings are the only creatures in the universe who have this sense of enjoyment. Human beings have been settled temporarily in the present world so that they may feel the pleasure of it and give thanks to God for it. One who shows his gratitude in this world will be settled in Paradise in the next world, where he will have perfect comfort and the fulfilment of his desires.

The present world is the place of temporary gratitude. This temporary gratitude is that which makes a person deserving of entry into eternal Paradise.

Remembrance and Prayer

As has been recorded in different books of ḥadīth, ʿĀʾishah said:

> *"The Prophet Muḥammad used to remember God on every occasion."* (Ṣaḥīḥ Muslim, Hadith No. 373)

This tradition does not relate to worship. Certain people describe it in the sense of the repetition of such words as Bismillāh, al-ḥamdu liʾllāh, in shāʾ Allāh, mā shāʾ Allāh, et alia. But this interpretation does not describe the real meaning of this tradition.

The fact is that remembrance and prayer are the expressions of the soul which has discovered and realized God. A person has to face different types of occasions in his life. If he has the thinking and learning ability, he will find that there is some aspect of remembrance of God on all occasions. By making these occasions points of reference he can transform them into a high level of remembrance and prayer. ʿĀʾishah found this very phenomenon in the life of the Prophet of Islam. She saw that the Prophet Muḥammad remembered God by making every occasion a point of reference.

The truth is that remembrance and prayer are not just the repetition of some standard words. Remembrance and prayer stem from different occasions and different circumstances which remind a person of God. In every experience he can see aspects of God's greatness. According to this heightened consciousness, the words that come spontaneously to the lips of such a person are called remembrance and prayer.

Prayer is Worship

There is a tradition which states that prayer (du'ā') is the real essence of worship (Sunan al-Tirmidhī, Hadith No. 3371) rather prayer is worship (Sunan al-Tirmidhī, Hadith No. 2969). This same truth has been set forth in the Qur'ān as well as in the ḥadīth. It is natural for prayer to be real worship. Indeed, when a believer discovers God with His perfect attributes, he also discovers his total worthlessness in comparison to God.

God is the Lord, I am His servant. God is the Giver, I am the taker. God is the All-Powerful and I am submissive and helpless. This feeling immediately makes the suppliant capable of prayer to God. Prayer is that greatest of relationships through which a believer comes close to God. Prayer is the source of connection between God and the believer. A person receives everything through prayer. All the forms of worship make a person capable of praying to God, so that he may become the receiver. For example, in the Qur'ān, after giving the command to fast in the month of Ramaḍān, the following verse says:

> *"When My servants ask you about Me, say that I am near. I respond to the call of one who calls, whenever he calls to Me: let them, then, respond to Me, and believe in Me, so that they may be rightly guided." (2:186)*

The same adjuration was expressed by Jesus Christ:

> *"Ask and it will be given to you; seek and you will find; knock and the door will be opened to you. For every one who asks receives; the one who seeks finds; and to the one who knocks, the door will be opened." (Matthew 7:7–8)*

Prayer is not just a few words: it is the greatest of actions just as a good deed is never fruitless, so also is true prayer never fruitless.

When a person prays sincerely, it means that he is placing himself in God's hands and when this happens, there is no one who can prevent his prayer from being fulfilled.

The Need for the Renewal of Faith

According to a ḥadīth, the Prophet of Islām once observed:

> *"Renew your faith." When asked how to do so, the Prophet replied, "renew your faith by the kalimah 'lā ilāha illā Allāh' (there is no god but one God)." (Musnad Aḥmad, Hadith No. 8710)*

From this tradition we learn that the kalimah is not something which should be recited only once in a lifetime, thinking that it would suffice for one's whole life. No indeed. Its renewal is necessary. The renewal of the kalimah means awakening the consciousness of faith again and again, so that a person does not become forgetful and lose his sensitivity to it. A person should always have a living active faith.

There is another aspect to this tradition that we learn from another tradition, and it is that Islām does away with all the things of the past. (Ṣaḥīḥ Muslim, Hadith No. 121) One aspect of it relates to that time when an individual recited the kalimah and became a believer. Another aspect pertains to later life. After bringing faith, it repeatedly happens that the individual makes mistakes. He feels then that he has become distanced from the mercy of God. At that time what the believer has to do is to have full faith in God being ever present and, in the presence of God, he should again recite the kalimah in solitude, with keen awareness. He should say,

> *"I witness that there is no God but the one God and I witness that Muḥammad is His servant and His Messenger." In addition to saying this, he should pray to God in this way, "O God, forgive my sins and envelope me with Your mercy once again. I have accepted Islām once again, so that I may join the body of the believers, and the virtuous.*

O God, I had digressed from the right path, so give me a
new life of faith and Islām once again."

Those who do so with keen awareness will keep receiving new faith. As a result of this renewed faith they will become, in the words of a tradition, like a newborn child. (Ṣaḥīḥ al-Bukhārī, Hadith No. 1521)

The Reality of the World

According to Abū Hurayrah:

"The Prophet Muḥammad said, the world is accursed and whatever is in the world, all are accursed, except remembrance of God and those things which are near to Him, and scholars and the seekers of knowledge." (Sunan al-Tirmidhī, Hadith No. 2322)

The world and remembrance of God are interrelated. To make this world a point of reference for remembrance of God is what has been called remembrance of God in this tradition. If this remembrance is in the name of God, it is direct remembrance of God. If someone remembers God without His name then it is indirect remembrance. Indeed the scholars and the seekers of knowledge desired by God are those who make their knowledge a source of remembrance of God.

God is the Creator of the world and also of the worldly things. That is why the world cannot be accursed. Actually, it is proper use or misuse of the world which makes it a boon or a curse. For one who forgets God after getting the world, this world is accursed and for one who gets the world as a source of remembrance of God, the world will prove to be a thing of mercy and a blessing for him.

The truth is that, the present world has been made as a testing ground. All the things in the world have the status of test papers. This is so because the failures and the successful can be separated from each other. One who takes worldly things to be food for the remembrance of God, succeeds in the test. On the contrary, one for whom worldly things distance him from God, fails in the test. In this way, depending upon whether we make proper use of the world or misuse it, determines whether the world is a curse or a blessing.

Small Thankfulness, Big Thankfulness

According to one tradition, the Prophet of Islām observed:

> *"One who is not thankful for getting small things will not be thankful for getting greater things." (Musnad Aḥmad, Hadith No. 18449)*

This ḥadīth of the Prophet tells of a law of nature. The law of nature is that by remembering a lesser event, events of greater importance are recalled.

Psychological studies tell us that there are many separate files in the human mind. For instance, the file of love, the file of hate, the file of acknowledgement, the file of oppression, etc. Data about all those things which are part of one's experience are constantly being filed away separately in the mind. When a person is impacted by some event, his mind is stimulated and the file on that subject is then immediately opened up and all the events of that nature get classified anew in the human mind.

This law of nature is of great importance in the matter of thankfulness and acknowledgement. For instance today you received a mobile, you spoke to someone some distance away, then you thought that earlier I was faced with such difficulty in making contact with someone who was far away, then with deep emotion, you thank God. At that point, your mind will be jogged. Then the file in the mind will be opened up in which all the items warranting thankfulness and acknowledgement that you have received throughout your entire life have been preserved. By this law of nature, it happens that even the small occasions for thankfulness become reminders of greater events when thankfulness was appropriate. In this way, smaller incidents of thankfulness become pointers to a greater degree of thankfulness, to the point where finally a spring of thankfulness overflows in a person's heart. This feeling of gratitude increases our attachment with God and ultimately causes us to reach the highest levels of realization.

A Life of Security

'Abdullāh ibn 'Umar reports this tradition of the Prophet:

> *"When the door of du'ā' (prayer) is opened to anyone of you, it is as if all the doors of divine mercy have been opened. The best du'ā' in the eyes of God is pertaining to health and security ('āfiyah)." (Sunan al-Tirmidhī, Hadith No. 3548)*

Du'ā' in actual fact is an expression of one's helplessness vis-à-vis God. The truest expression of helplessness is produced only by complete acknowledgement of the greatness of God. As a result of the discovery of God's greatness, the feeling of total helplessness is born within one. Performing a du'ā' is, in actual fact, a way of expressing one's feeling of helplessness.

'Āfiyah means a life of freedom from illness and a peaceful life in the world. In worldly life health and peace are undoubtedly the greatest blessings of God. To excel in anything one needs this kind of 'āfiyah. Finding a life of health and security is not a human achievement; it is bestowed on an individual by God. It is because of this importance of 'āfiyah that a person should keep praying to God for it.

'Āfiyah (well-being) has nothing to do with wealth or material sources of comfort. 'Āfiyah relates entirely to mental peace. This mental peace is granted to a person by special divine blessing. A person can truly engage in the remembrance of God, du'ā', worship and God-realization only when he is blessed with a life of peace and security. In this case, it would be right to say that the greatest thing that we should ask of God is 'āfiyah, rather than wealth or material comforts.

Closeness to God in Every Situation

According to one of the traditions of the Prophet of Islām,

"God offered to turn the whole valley of Makkah into gold for me. I said, 'No, O My Lord! I rather want that one day I should have my fill and another day I should go hungry. And when I go hungry I entreat You and remember You and the day I have my fill, I praise You and am thankful to You." (Musnad Aḥmad, Hadith No. 22190)

The truth is that states of faith relate to circumstances. In life, whenever any situation arises, it accordingly provides a believer with some "food" for his faith. All states of faith ensue from particular situations. Man has been placed in the present world in order to put him to the test, that is why all kinds of situations are faced by every man and woman. This happens so that it may be seen who has passed the test and who has not.

In this world, states of comfort and pain and pleasure are relative. Regardless of the state, what is actually important is whether those involved gave the desired response; whether the response they gave was positive or negative. So it is one's response rather than that of the force of circumstances which is of significance. Once this reality is clear to people, their focus will be on the response to the coming situation, rather than on the comfort or the problems arising from it. That is, whether their response was one of gratitude or ingratitude, one of patience or impatience. An individual must introspect in every situation, rather than complain about external circumstances.

Conscious Worship

'Abdullāh ibn 'Umar narrates that the Prophet once observed:

"Man apparently performs ṣalāh, fasting, zakāh, ḥajj, and 'umrah." The Prophet went on to mention all the good acts, then he said, "But on the Day of Judgement he will be rewarded in accordance with his reason or

*understanding (ʿaql)." (Shuʿab al-Īmān, al-Bayhaqī,
Hadith No. 4316)*

In this ḥadīth, the word ʿaql is used in the sense of understanding. In this tradition ʿaql means what we may call consciousness. And the ḥadīth means that if a person engages in the remembrance of God and His worship, he will be rewarded for his acts not by measuring the quantity but by gauging the quality. The reward for all these acts will be given as is commensurate with their spirit. One who has worshipped with full consciousness will be fittingly rewarded.

For instance, a person performs some form of worship but that worship according to the Qur'ān is done in a state of absent-mindedness. So, apparently, he is engaged in acts of worship but, so far as mental awareness is concerned, his focus is elsewhere. Such a person does the worship which is not desirable. The requisite form of worship is one in which a person is in a state which has been expressed thus in the Qur'ān:

> *"The true believers are those whose hearts tremble with awe at the mention of God" (8:2)*

and

> *"their worship causes the skins of those in awe of their Lord to creep." (39:23)*

Such a believer worships with full consciousness. All the great rewards will be given by God to those who have performed worship with full consciousness.

To attain this high state of worship, an individual must refrain from distracting himself with irrelevant things and must always keep praying to God for the progress of his faith.

Invoking God's Mercy

Prayer is no simple matter, prayer is to invoke God, calling upon Him to exert His powers. Without doubt, we can say that when a true prayer comes out of the lips of a helpless person, it is akin to a challenge to God's honour. When a helpless person becomes a true seeker and raises his hand in prayer before God, he makes his problem God's own problem. At that time, it is not possible for God to send him away empty-handed. This is the reality which has been expressed in one particular tradition of the Prophet. (Sunan al-Tirmidhī, Hadith No. 3556)

One way of praying is to learn some words of prayer by rote and keep repeating them as a ritual in order to ask God to grant us the best of this world and the best of the next world. Another more effective way of praying is to make some event the point of reference of the prayer. For instance, during the British era, there was a Collector in Lucknow, by the name of Siddique Hasan (ICS). He once arrested a dacoit called Sukhwa and locked him up in a room in his large bungalow, where he himself was staying. It was a very severe winter. At night, Siddique Hasan went out to take a round, when Sukhwa saw him. He said: "Sir, your Sukhwa is getting very cold." On hearing this, Siddique Hasan went to his room, picked up his own blanket and gave it to Sukhwa.

Sukhwa was a criminal but he was a helpless person when he was arrested. The Collector seeing his helplessness separated his criminality from his helplessness and treated him sympathetically. If some servant of God makes a supplication such as:

> "O God may You also treat me similarly sympathetically
> in spite of my having committed many wrongs. O God,
> ignore those errors of mine and deal mercifully with me,
> a helpless person."

For one who prays in such a manner, it is quite possible that God will accept his entreaties and forgive him.

The Safeguarding of the Feeling of Gratitude

The Prophet of Islām once observed:

> "Look only to those who are less great than you; do not look
> to those who are greater than you, because in this way you

will not undervalue God's blessings upon you." (Musnad Aḥmad, Hadith No. 10246)

This ḥadīth is explained by another ḥadīth.

"The Prophet once said that God will accept him as His thankful and patient servant who possesses two particular qualities. One is the capacity, in the matters of this world, to look to those who are inferior to him and then be thankful to God for the blessings that God has given him. The other is the capacity in matters of religion, to look to those who are superior to him and then to follow them. But one who in matters of religion looks to those who are inferior to him while one who in matters of this world looks to those who are greater than him and then he is sorrowful about what he is lacking in, will neither be a thankful servant, nor a patient servant in the eyes of God." (Sunan al-Tirmidhī, Hadith No. 2512)

Gratitude is the greatest form of worship. What is most required of a person is that he should discover God as the greatest Benefactor. Then his heart and mind should be filled with the awareness of God's blessings. He must recognize God as a Being, who is raining down His countless blessings upon him. This consciousness should be so strong that in no way should the feelings of gratefulness to God be absent from his heart.

But this is no simple matter. To keep oneself brimming with feelings of thankfulness, it is essential that a person's consciousness should be fully alive. He should take special care to perpetuate his gratefulness. He should not give any place in his heart to such sentiments as may be harmful to his feeling of thanksgiving. He may tolerate anything except the erosion of feelings of thankfulness. It is natural that in the present world it happens inevitably that there are people who are not equal in everything. As such, a person feels that in material matters, some have less and some have more. But if a person compares himself with someone who has apparently more than him, he will develop an inferiority complex and his feeling of thankfulness will get eroded. Therefore one should not compare himself or herself with those who are apparently, materially, better placed than him or her. What a person should do rather is compare himself with those who are materially less well off than he is. In this way, his feeling of thanksgiving will remain alive. His heart will never be bereft of the awareness of God's blessings.

In the present world it is inevitable that there should be inequality. Some have more and some have less, some are left behind, some forge ahead, and some have more power while some are weak. All these differences are due to the exigencies of people being put to the test. The process of testing requires that a person should be faced with different kinds of circumstances, but without allowing himself to be influenced by those circumstances, he should keep the consciousness of his faith alive.

In spite of adverse circumstances, his feeling of thankfulness should not be lessened. He should pass through untoward situations without losing the virtue of acknowledgement. This should be so, even when he is having such experiences as produce negative feelings. He should even then keep himself thinking positively. Thanksgiving is a human being's most precious offering to his Lord. Wise is he who does not allow his feelings of thankfulness to be eroded even in the most unfavourable of situations.

The Greatest Prayer

The greatest prayer is one which is said with a genuine point of reference: death is the greatest such point of reference. One who is aware of this can sincerely take the great name of God in prayer.

What is death? Death is not the end of life. It is rather the end of one's stay on our present earth. Here, everything is provided for one's survival. When death comes, what happens is that all of a sudden the dying person is deprived of the present planet earth. But what he received on the planet earth, was, in reality, not the result of his striving, but rather an unconditional gift from God. Man takes everything for granted, therefore, he remains unaware of this reality. But if a person realizes that all the things in this world are divine gifts, this discovery will become a great point of reference for him in his prayer.

One who consciously discovers this reality will call out:

> *"O God, even when I was totally helpless, You, out of your boundless mercy, gave me everything without my having deserved them. Again after death I will find myself totally helpless. O God, in the way You compensated for my helplessness before death, may You compensate fully for my helplessness in the life after death also, and give me in greater measure all the things You previously gave me in the life before death."*

Praying for salvation in the afterlife is, without doubt, to invoke the greatness of God. Fortunate are those who are able to pray in such a manner for that is what is acceptable to God.

Discover the Reasons for Thankfulness

If you eat tasty food and then you say al-ḥamdu li'llāh (praise be to God), this is a very low level of thanksgiving, for it is based on observation and taste, and is not on a high plane of thanksgiving.

The high level of thanksgiving which befits man is when food is placed before him, he is reminded of the entire creative system. He thinks that all these food items were formerly raw materials. By a very superior process God converted these into food. In this way, through a universal process, all these food items came into existence.

Then he starts thinking that all these food items, in their initial form, could not be a source of energy for himself. Therefore, God went further and created a very complex digestive system. This is an automatic system of digestion. Whenever you eat anything, this digestive system miraculously converts these food items into living cells; these living things are then converted into flesh and blood in the body. On thinking like this, such an ocean of thanksgiving wells up within you that you fail to find words to express your intense feelings.

From this example, one can understand what is a lower level of thanksgiving (shukr) and what is a higher level of thanksgiving. If you give thanks on a basic level, you will always live in ungratefulness. For a high level of gratitude you need to give thanks on a noble human level. But these are the things which are least found in the world (The Qur'ān, 34:13). The kind of gratitude God desires from a human being is always on a higher level. A lower level of thanksgiving is not acceptable from humans.

Thanksgiving is an Act of Sacrifice

Thanksgiving is the greatest form of worship. Indeed the price of Paradise is gratitude. Without gratitude, faith cannot be depended upon. Without gratitude, there is no true worship. Without gratitude man cannot experience those noble feelings which have been described in the Qur'ān as "being devoted servants of God." (3:79) The truth is that the genuine spirit of religiosity is thanksgiving. Without thanksgiving, or gratitude, religiosity is just like the outer peel of a fruit.

But just uttering some words of thanksgiving is not all there is to gratitude. Gratitude is an act of sacrifice—rather the greatest sacrifice. Only those who are ready to make that great sacrifice can experience the thanksgiving as desired by God.

The truth is that, in the present world, a person in some way or the other, is a prey to the feeling of deprivation. Every person has some negative feelings about this in his heart. Every man and woman starts living a life of hatred and complaint for various reasons. This is the state of affairs which makes gratitude the most difficult thing for an individual. A person may utter words of gratitude, but his heart is totally free from the true feelings of thanksgiving.

In such a situation only that person can engage in the act of thanksgiving whose consciousness is so awakened that in spite of feeling he has reasons for ungratefulness, is nevertheless grateful. He is one who, living in a jungle of negative thoughts, still lives with positive feelings. He should rid himself of all the things which are obstacles to thanksgiving, and should create within himself the real feelings of gratitude.

Thanksgiving is the kind of worship which is desirable in every situation. One who thinks that thanksgiving is only for when he has got something which he wanted and that the things he received were in accordance with his desire, can never be a true thanksgiver. True thanksgiving to God can be done only by those who learn the secret of thanksgiving in spite of having complaints.

The Great Prayer

Prayer literally means to call upon, that is, the servant with the full sense of his servitude to his Lord, calls upon his Lord. This prayer is of two kinds. The general kind of prayer is to repeat the set words of prayers and call upon God in terms of those words.

Another kind of du'a' is what is called the great prayer. This prayer expresses those deep feelings of servitude in a person that he starts calling upon God in such words as invoke God's mercy.

For instance, there is a prayer which is set forth thus in the Qur'ān:

> *"Our Lord, grant us good in this world as well as good
> in the world to come, and protect us from the torment of
> the fire." (2:201)*

When you recite this prayer a deep sense of servitude will be awakened in you. Then you will remember all those blessings of God which He has given you in the present world. Then with a trembling heart, you will say, "O God, You have not deprived me of the good things of this world, then give me the good things of the Hereafter as well, or do not deprive me of the good things of the Hereafter as well."

Similarly, when you study the sacred ḥadīth in which God says:

*"I am with My servant's expectations, so the servant
ought to have good expectations with Me." (Dhakhīrah
al-Ḥuffāẓ, Ibn al-Qaysarānī, Hadith No. 6541)*

On reading this ḥadīth, you will remember those blessings which God has given you in this world. You will be moved and these words will come to your lips, "O God, in this world, You have given me the best in every respect, so in the Hereafter also give me the best in every respect" – this is an example of great prayer. Blessed are those who are granted this great prayer.

Prayer: Verbal Form of Spiritual Experience

Prayer is a discovery. When a person discovers his helplessness and the power of prayer, he is so greatly moved that the words that spontaneously spring to his lips is prayer. Prayer gives verbal shape to spiritual experiences, and, thus, internal feelings find external expression. The effect of prayer relates not to words but to one who prays and to his internal feelings. For instance, prayer happens spontaneously when a person ponders upon or thinks about God's blessings and that God in giving him the whole life support system, has acted unilaterally.

On thinking of these things, he remembers the period after death since what he has received in this world has been given to him in order to put him to the test. What will happen in the phase after death is entirely in the hands of God. On the one hand, he discovers his helplessness and on the other, he discovers God's power. Then, thinking about all these things he becomes agitated and these words come to his lips, "O God, by Your grace, extend Your blessings from this world to the next world."

There is prayer and then there is what goes before prayer. The real prayer is uttered when there has been a prior spiritual experience. Man thinks of his Creator, of his Lord. As a result of this deep thinking, spiritual activity is engendered within his heart and mind. His inner state, entering a revolutionary phase, becomes excited and he starts experiencing spiritual realities. He starts feeling that, at an internal level, contact with higher realities has been established and when this non-verbal feeling in his inner self finds expression in words, that is prayer or du'ā'.

Experience and Prayer

I once heard a story related by an announcer on All India Radio. It was about a man in London, who was looking for a job. He applied to several companies and institutions but failed to get a job. Finally, he thought of a unique strategy. He wrote on a placard 'Please give me a job', and holding this placard aloft, he stood out on a street in London. It started raining, but he just kept standing there. That evening, a timber merchant of London who was passing along that street read the words on the placard. He got out of his car, came up to the man and gave him his card. He said, "Come to my office tomorrow, and I'll give you a job." And the very next day the man got a job.

When I heard the story on the radio I felt a great unease. I was reminded of death, of the Hereafter, and of Paradise. Then I prayed to God: "Please give me a seat in Paradise."

This is a simple example of how an experience can be turned into a point of reference. It is a fact that while leading our lives in the present world, we have different kinds of experiences, almost on a daily basis. If our mind is awakened and we have attained realization of God, all these experiences or events can become points of reference for us. As a result of these experiences and events, the realized soul, the believer will remember God. Prayers full of devotion will keep coming to his lips. He may be living in the material world, but it is this material world which will become a source of spiritual provision for him.

Living Prayer

Once on an international journey, I had to stay at Frankfurt airport, where I was told by a lady officer that since I did not have a German visa, they could not arrange my stay in some hotel in the city. Anyway, she took me to a part of the airport where I could lie down. Then she brought food on a tray and also gave me a blanket. She told me I could rest there. And in the morning, she added, she would come and take me to my next flight. After eating the food, I lay down and wrapped myself up in the blanket. Then, in the morning when that lady came back again, I wanted to give the blanket back to her, but she said there was no need to give it back.

When I remember this event, it becomes a point of reference for me. I say, "O God, in my life in this world, You have given me everything. Will You deprive me of everything in the life after death? Please, in the life after death, continue to show me the mercy which I received in the life before death. In the life before death, You saved me from all deprivations. Please, also in the life after death, save me from all deprivation. When a human being does not want to take back the things that he has given one, then how can You, the Creator of man, take back what You have given me in this world?"

When one thinks in this way in a keen state of awareness, every event of this life will become a point of reference for God's remembrance and prayer. By referring to every event he starts remembering God. Every event will become such a point of reference as will inspire him to find new words for prayer. This is true remembrance of God. When a person can have such feelings, he becomes like a tree whose greenery never dries up, and which keeps giving a yield of flowers and fruits for all eternity.

A Point of Reference

The greatest prayer (du'ā') is one which is said with a point of reference, that is to say on the basis of an experience which causes you to remember God. At that moment, a spiritual storm is brought about within you, and with this, some words of prayer (du'ā') come to your lips. This prayer to God has great significance and as such is very important. This is the prayer which is described in the ḥadīth as being said in the great name of God.

For instance, on a very hot day in summer, you visit someone's house. When you arrive, he ushers you into his home with honour and brings cold water in a glass. You drink the water, then your parched throat is moistened, and your thirst is quenched.

After this experience you have another spiritual storm within you. You exclaim, "O God! Similarly, one day I have to come to You. When I met a person (in the world) created by You he offered me a glass of cold water. Then would You, the Creator, ask Your angel to bring boiling water for me to drink (in the Hereafter)?"

The genuine prayer is not a mere repetition of certain words. In a real prayer the words are only symbolic. The real prayer is one which is said with God-realization. The real prayer is one in which the words come to your lips after a discovery of God. This real prayer is a superior form of worship.

The real prayer is one which brings God's servant closer to his Creator. The servant's whole existence finds expression in the words of his prayer.

The Discovery of One's Helplessness

Man is totally a helpless creature: that is how he was created. But due to the exigencies of his being put to the test, his helplessness is, apparently, covered with a veil of power. What man has to do is to tear asunder this cover, even when ostensibly in possession of power. In that way he will discover his own helplessness. This discovery is without doubt the greatest discovery he can make. It is in this discovery that the secret of all blessings is hidden.

The discovery of helplessness is the greatest discovery for a human being. This greatest of discoveries affords man a unique opportunity for remembrance of God, or prayer to God. Moreover, this discovery gives a person the occasion to say to God, "O God! You have created me in a state of utter helplessness. On the one hand, is your Omnipotence and, on the other hand, is man's total helplessness. This being so, You cannot remain indifferent to man's predicament. It would not befit Your Majesty and Your divine Glory to have a relationship between You and man of total human helplessness and indifference on Your part. Between God and man there must be such a bond as exists between a deprived one and the Giver. Such a relationship befits the Glory and Majesty of God."

This is the prayer which has been described in a tradition as a prayer taking the great name of God. When a servant of God says with sincerity: "O God! You have created man in total helplessness, so now you cannot remain indifferent to man's situation," God's mercy comes faster than the speed of light.

How to Overcome Tension

Faith in God gives a person the greatest support in this world. Belief in God is the greatest source of strength. A Persian poet once said:

> *Dushman agar qavī ast, nigahbān qavītar ast*
> *(If the problem is great, the problem solver is greater).*

The present world is fraught with problems. Here every man and woman has to live with problems. Repeatedly they are confronted with such situations as cause them to feel helpless.

During life's journey, a person repeatedly feels that the road ahead is closed. Repeatedly he is beset by negative feelings. He feels that he has exhausted all his means and resources; that he cannot solve his problems on his own. This is a delicate situation and that is when he calls upon his Lord. At that moment, the Lord answers his prayers and raises him up out of his state of helplessness.

On such occasions, one who does not believe in God falls victim to despair. He becomes disheartened. He loses the courage to go ahead in life. Reaching an impasse, one starts living in a state of tension. And tension is at the root of all diseases. The truth is that there is no problem greater for an individual than this.

But one who has full faith in God, never falls a prey to frustration. In all situations, he is convinced that God will certainly come to his rescue. Such a person remains fully convinced that God will certainly come to his aid even when everyone else has deserted him.

Learning Lessons from Loss

When I performed my ḥajj in 1982, I was accompanied on the journey by an Arab professor. Our plane landed at Jeddah airport and then both of us left for Makkah. On reaching Makkah, my Arab companion realized all of a sudden that he had forgotten his handbag which contained 20,000 Saudi Riyals at the Jeddah airport. Leaving me at Makkah, he immediately went back to look for his handbag. After he had left, I said two units of prayer. When I raised my hands in prayer, these words came to my lips: "O God, turn this incident into a lesson for us. Do not make it a loss for us."

Man ought, of course, to make every effort to avoid making mistakes or incurring losses. But, when he has already suffered a loss, the most important thing for him to do is to refrain from grieving over it. Once an error has been made, it is like an arrow shot from a bow, never to return. Instead of weeping and wailing over the loss, one should pray to God to save one from its evil consequences.

Not making any mistakes is good. But making a mistake can also be good when the consciousness of having made a mistake causes one to turn towards God. Such a mistake becomes a cause for worship and the one in error begins praying to God. According to a tradition of the Prophet,

> *"Prayer is worship." (Sunan al-Tirmidhī, Hadith No. 2969)*

Grieving over a loss is like living in the loss. But turning to God after a loss is like seeking compensation for it. And undoubtedly God has the power to turn losses into greater gains.

There are two aspects of every loss. One is the loss itself and the other is the learning of a lesson from it. In the case of any loss, one should do just that—learn a lesson from it. In this way, loss will turn into gain.

Universal Thanksgiving

You may have often heard people say, "I am thankful to God that I have my own house in the city and I am thankful to God that He has given me children. I am thankful to God that I have my own business. I am thankful to God that I have two cars, and so on." This kind of thanksgiving is minimal. This kind of gratitude cannot become like a river which flows on and on, whereas that gratitude which God wants should continue flowing in your hearts like rivers and oceans.

When such great thanksgiving is done, it is produced when you have that feeling of extended gratitude, indicating that you are not just focusing on your own self but are rather able to associate yourself with other human beings. When you think in this way, only then is that high quality of gratitude engendered which may be called universal thanksgiving.

When a son makes very good progress, his father is very happy to see this, because in his son's progress he sees his own progress. If the son is in America and making great progress and the father is in India, even despite such a great distance between them he is still happy to hear the news of his son's progress.

Moreover, if you want great gratitude to well up in your heart you shall have to associate with all of humanity. In such a situation, the progress of other human beings will start appearing as if it is your own progress. When regarding personal blessings, you feel a minor degree of gratitude, if you associate yourself with the whole of humanity then a billion, trillion degrees of thankfulness will arise within you. If formerly, there was just a drop of thanksgiving in your heart, you will now start feeling that a whole sea of gratitude is flowing within your heart.

The Discovery of Divine Blessings

Man has been granted numerous blessings from God. The greatest form of worship for man is to acknowledge these blessings. Thanksgiving is in fact such an acknowledgement. Thanksgiving is without doubt the greatest religious act, whereas not thanking God is quite the reverse. It is irreligious.

Nothing announces all these divine blessings as such. For instance, the global supply of oxygen is perpetual. But man has never had this announced to him. There are many such divine blessings as are received by man at all times. But this whole process goes on without mention.

In such a situation, how should a person express his gratitude or acknowledgement as an act of worship? There is only one way of doing so. That is, one should continue to discover God's blessings through contemplation.

Thanksgiving follows on naturally after discovering one's blessings. One who never makes such a discovery will certainly never be able to show any gratitude.

That is why such great importance is attached to reflection in the Traditions. According to one tradition:

> *"There is no worship equal to reflection." (Shu'ab al-Īmān, al-Bayhaqī, Hadith No. 4326)*

Contemplation means serious thinking. The act of thinking takes place in the mind, and is the source of all our actions. The more one thinks, the deeper the meaning which will be discovered by him. The same is true of thanksgiving. It is only by thinking that anyone discovers God's limitless blessings.

With this discovery one's heart and mind brim over with gratitude. The greater the sense of discovery the greater the degree of thanksgiving. It is contemplation that leads one to discovery and to elevated levels of thanksgiving.

How to Find Spiritual Food

One professor gave me the good news that the tenure of his service period had expired so he was going to retire, but since the university had given him two year extension, his service would continue for two more years.

When I heard the news of his extension, it became for me a point of reference for saying a prayer. I said, "O God, You have created me and unilaterally have given me all the things I needed for life support. Death will put an end to all these blessings but, if You desire, You can grant me a further extension. Man may grant only a limited period of extension, but You are the Lord of the World. If you so desire, You can grant an unlimited period of extension. You may cause this extension to last for all eternity."

A person leads his life in the midst of all sorts of happenings and experiences. If he ponders upon things and keeps his mind awakened, every event and every experience will become a source of spiritual food for him. He will find some point of reference in every event, in every experience by referring to which he may engage in remembrance of God and may utter such words of heartfelt prayer as may be acceptable to God.

Just as the study of books is a source of spiritual food for a person, similarly incidents and experiences also provide sources of spiritual food. One who develops the ability to derive lessons from them, will find that his life's journey will become a source of such spiritual development as lasts right till his death.

True Action and True Prayer

After spending a short time on earth, everyone born into this world is going to die. Subsequently, all men and women shall have to appear before God. Then God will decide upon everyone's eternal future, which will be either Paradise or Hell.

Salvation will be attainable by those who have pleased God by living their lives in a principled way, having engaged in right action and true prayer. The criterion of right action is that it is performed purely for the sake of God. And the criterion of true prayer is that it is said with the consciousness of being totally helpless.

Spiritually ennobled are those whose lives are graced by righteousness. The same can be said of those who can rid themselves of hypocrisy and never have double standards. The deeds of those who can save themselves from being morally weak are a reflection of their entire personalities. Their good conduct stems from right thinking. There is no discrepancy between intention and action. Moreover, those who have developed their consciousness to such a degree that, vis-à-vis the total power of God they acknowledge their state of helplessness, are granted the blessings of true prayer.

The truth is that true prayer and right action are not separate from each other. Good deeds are closely linked with true prayer. Psychologically, no distinction can be made between true prayer and right action.

Thanksgiving as Opposed to Arrogance

If, when you find something good, some blessing from God, and you consider it to be the result of your own struggle, of your own hard work or of your innate ability, you will become consumed by arrogance. But if you think that the blessings you have received are from God, you will have a sense of gratefulness. The former state or feeling results from deviation from the straight path, while the latter feeling results from the acceptance of true guidance.

The present world has been created for the purpose of putting a human being to the test. All events, without doubt take place at the Lord's behest. But all of these events have been shrouded in a veil of cause and effect. A person will pass the divine test only if he is able to tear asunder the apparent veil of cause and effect, for it is only then that he will arrive at true faith in God.

When you have a desire for something, you make an effort to find it.

Your efforts pass through various stages. Sometimes you apply your mind, sometimes you use your physical abilities, and sometimes you spend your wealth on it. Apparently, you reach your goal by passing through various stages of cause and effect.

Now if you view things, only by looking at appearances, you will regard success as a result of your own efforts. But if you have such insight as enables you to see things in depth, you will know all events come about through the instrumentality of God: they are not your own personal feats. It is this point on which an individual is being tested. Now it is incumbent upon a person that he tears asunder the apparent veil and goes deeper into the reality. Apparently, it would be, at his instance that things were happening, but he has to recognize that, in fact, everything happened at the behest of God.

Those who develop such insight have attained God-realization. Whereas those who do not prove to be men of insight will never attain God-realization.

The Reason behind Negative Mentality

In daily conversation, people regularly fall to complaining. When you talk to anyone, everyone will speak in the language of complaint. Everyone will talk in the most negative terms. The most common complaints are targeted at some person or some nation or some human group. This happens with people everywhere—this is the attitude which has made people turn away from any feeling of gratitude to God.

Indeed, all those incidents which people refer to in their grouses are man-made. But they form even less than 1% of the entire human life. Other events which can be called God-made, add up to more than 99%.

Keeping in view this difference, if you think deeply, you will find that those incidents which account for less than 1% are the main subject of conversation, but it is on that small percentage that people form their opinions. It is extraordinary that the divine bounties or blessings which a person has received and is continually receiving and which account for more than 99% of the happenings in his life, are not the subject of talk. When people do not think about these things, how are they to acknowledge them?

This is the real reason for the people's negative mentality. People take note only of human events and that is why they talk in negative terms. On the contrary, if they were aware of divine events, they would find that human events would become unworthy of any mention at all. If this were to happen, people would certainly forget about human complaints. They would be so enthralled by thinking of divine blessings that they would not even remember that someone had done something worthy of complaint. This is the kind of thinking which creates the true spirit in which we spontaneously say al-ḥamdu li'llāh (Praise be to God).

Love for Humanity

Everyone knows that the greatest credit goes to his parents in the building of his life. In this respect everyone keeps praising his parents. But such men and women are hard to find who know that the whole of humanity has played a part in the building of their lives. In this matter if parents play just one percent part, the general humanity plays 99% part. But no one knows this reality, no one acknowledges it.

For instance when you eat bread, your parent's role in this is less than 1%, while the role of the humanity in general is that of 99%. For, over a long civilizational process spanning thousands of years, it has become possible that a person may discover bread, as we know it today, and make it as his food. The same is the case of other things, for instance, clothes, houses, transport, machines, industries, etc.

The truth is that the things one possesses, one part of it is the direct gift, while the other part is the indirect gift. If the direct gift is akin to the tip of the iceberg then the indirect gift is akin to the iceberg. The indirect gift, apparently, is not visible but in its quantity it is much more than the direct gift. People know only the direct gift, that is why they are able to give very little thanks, they are not able to acknowledge as is due. Had they known the benefit of the indirect gift, their gratitude and acknowledgement will increase. They will start loving the whole humanity just like they love their parents.

The greatest form of worship for a person is to offer abundant gratefulness and abundant acknowledgement, but the person who is unaware of this reality will remain deprived of the worship of abundant thanksgiving and abundant acknowledgement.

Gratitude towards Others

A seminar held in the Mir Taqi Mir Hall at Jamia Millia Islamia on September 17, 2008, on the subject of 'Muslim Problems' was attended by educated Muslims, both religious and secular (including myself). Throughout the entire programme, which was conducted in English, all the speakers had something or the other negative to say about the state of the Muslims and, without exception, all of them represented Muslims as a community subjected to persecution. One even said that Indian Muslims were 'under siege'.

It made me very sad to hear all this. I was reminded of my first visit to Delhi in 1943, when I came to see Jamia for the first time and met the Vice Chancellor, Dr. Zakir Ḥusain (d. 1969). At that time Jamia had the appearance of an ordinary college. Being unrecognized, its degree had no value in the job market. Today, after a period of 75 years, we find a full-fledged, central university by the name of Jamia Millia Islamia. All this progress has been made in post-independence India.

The seminar was held in a large, modern hall, equipped with all the latest cutting edge facilities. In such an environment, the speakers should rather have stressed on the fact that the tremendous progress made by Jamia symbolized the continuous progress that Muslims were making in this country. This is a state of affairs which should elicit gratitude. Then why is it that the participants sounded so ungrateful even when they were speaking in such a highly developed Muslim institution? My thinking was that people were not afraid of God, otherwise, according to a tradition of the Prophet, they ought to fear that if feelings of gratefulness to others were lacking in them, they would also be deprived of feelings of gratefulness towards God. And without doubt the deprivation of feelings of gratitude to God is the greatest possible deprivation.

This reality has been expressed in the following tradition of the Prophet: "One who is not thankful to man, cannot be thankful to God either." (Musnad Aḥmad, Hadith No. 11280).

Acknowledgement of God's Glory

The first phase of Islam witnessed an extraordinary expansion of the Islamic Caliphate, but despite the vastness of its area, up to the time of the Umayyads, the centre of the Caliphate was only one, and that was Damascus. After the Abbasid revolution, a separate Sultanate was established in Andalusia. Thus, there came into existence two centres of the Muslim empire. Soon thereafter an independent political centre was established in Morocco. Then followed an independent rule in Egypt. In this way, one after another, independent Muslim states came into existence. A vast empire was divided into smaller Muslim kingdoms. One of these Muslim Sultanates is known as the Samanids. The Samanid Sultanate was established in Iran and lasted for about 150 years.

Naṣr ibn Aḥmad ibn Sāmān (d. 892) was a Samanid ruler. It is said that when he conquered Nishapur he arranged for a big celebration. When he sat on his throne, he asked a certain ʿālim (religious scholar) to recite some verses from the Qurʾān on the occasion of his coronation. The ʿālim recited the appropriate verses from chapter 40, one of which was as follows: "To whom shall the kingdom belong that Day? It shall belong to God, the One, the All Powerful." (40:16)

When the ʿālim recited this verse, Sultan Naṣr ibn Aḥmad trembled with fear of God. He came down from his throne, took off his crown and prostrated himself before God. He said: "O my Lord, undoubtedly the kingdom is Yours, not mine."

The superior qualities of prayer or the high quality of remembrance of God has nothing to do with mere recitation of words, but has rather to do with the inner states of the suppliant. According to a ḥadīth, "One who humbles himself is the one who is held by God to be deserving of honour." (Ṣaḥīḥ Muslim, Hadith No. 2588). He is the person who is able, by the grace of God, to remember God and pray to Him in such a way as to invoke His mercy and blessing, and it is as if one who is blessed with such prayer has attained Paradise on this earth itself.

Remembering God in Solitude

Prayer means calling upon God. Such prayer is a great form of worship. According to a ḥadīth, prayer is worship. (Sunan al-Tirmidhī, Hadith No. 2969; Sunan Ibn Mājah, Hadith No. 3828). According to another ḥadīth, prayer is the kernel of worship (Sunan al-Tirmidhī, Hadith No. 3771).

Prayer is an act of a very personal nature. Everyone has to pray for himself on his own, just as everyone performs his own worship. No one tells another person to pray in his stead.

According to chapter 32 of the Qur'ān, this is one of the virtues of believers: "They forsake their beds, calling upon their Lord in fear and in hope, and spend out of what We have provided them with." (32:16) That is, they call upon their Lord in fear and hope. Calling upon God in this way is an extremely personal thing. Such prayer emerges from the deepest recesses of one's heart. This kind of prayer has to be done by the individual himself. He cannot ask someone to fear God for him or to trust in God for him. Prayer is a criterion of a person's servitude. One who believes in God must experience such moments in his life when his soul is moved greatly by the remembrance of God; when his heart and mind experience great convulsions in reflecting upon the concept of God. It is then that with this heightened spiritual state of mind he begins to entreat God, to pray with heartfelt words.

One in whom this feeling does not arise will not, as regards his faith in God, be held to be reliable in the eyes of God. According to a ḥadīth: "One who does not beseech God, invites the wrath of God." (Sunan al-Tirmidhī, Hadith No. 3373).

Prayer is an act of great delicacy which takes place between God and man. During this act, no third person exists. It is a fact that the best prayer is that in which one pours out one's heart in solitude. According to a tradition, "One virtue of such a believer is that of remembering God in solitude and then his eyes filling with tears." (Ṣaḥīḥ al-Bukhārī, Hadith No. 660).

When looked at in the light of the Qur'ān and ḥadīth, we learn that prayer is a sublime act of a very personal nature. For every believer, it is an expression of his godly feelings. It is only when you keep this reality before you that you realize that prayer is not something that a senior person should be asked to do for you. Such a request would produce an invalid form of prayer. It is like going to man instead of to God. Similarly, praying on a loud speaker is also lacking in seriousness. Such prayer is not true prayer. Learning some words by rote and keeping on repeating them is also not prayer. Prayer, in reality, is an act which moves your heart intensely: it is not the recitation of a combination of some ritual words.

In Ṣaḥīḥ al-Bukhārī, there is a maxim which reads: "Your prayer is your faith." (Ṣaḥīḥ al-Bukhārī, Kitāb al-Īmān, ch. 1) This means that just as your faith is, so will your prayer be. Prayer is a criterion by which to judge your faith.

If a person achieves a deeper level of faith, his prayer will also come out of the deeper recesses of his heart, and will have a very spiritual colour to it. When one prays in this manner, his whole existence will become a part of his prayer. Prayer for him will become a meeting point with God. It will be like conversing in whispers with God. (Ṣaḥīḥ Muslim, Hadith No. 551). On the contrary, for one whose faith has not become a part of his heart, prayer will be nothing but verbal repetition of certain words. It will amount to reiterating certain words ritualistically and this has nothing to do with the feelings of the heart. Such prayer will only be the utterance of mere words and not an expression of spiritual states.

Chapter 05

ATTRIBUTES OF GOD

The Attributes and the Great Name of God

The Quran tells us:

"God has the most excellent names." (7:180).

This has been mentioned at three other places in the scriptures.

"His are the finest names" (17:110).

"His are the most excellent names" (20:8).

"His are the most excellent names" (59:24).

Here, "names" have the extended meaning of attributes, that is, all the best attributes inhere specifically in God.

How many divine attributes are there? We learn from a hadith that they number 99. Some scholars say there is a greater number, i.e., about one thousand (Tafsīr Ibn Kathīr, vol. 2, p. 269). But the issue of number here is relative to the limitations of the human vocabulary. The words in human language are finite, while the being of God is infinite. God's attributes are, therefore, in reality unlimited. The ninety nine best names are, as it were, a major sampling of God's infinity of attributes.

The Ninety Nine Names of God

There is a tradition which has been recorded in different books of Hadith.

> *According to Ṣaḥīḥ al-Bukhārī: "Abū Hurayra has recorded that the Prophet of Islam observed—God has ninety nine names, one less than a hundred. Those who have counted these words will enter Paradise." (Ṣaḥīḥ al-Bukhārī, Hadith No. 2736)*

In this tradition of the Prophet, reference is made to the enumeration of the best names of God. This realization must be at a conscious level rather than at the level of counting the beads on the rosary.

These names of God are, in actual fact, different aspects of the attributes of God. When a person reflects on the existence of God and His creations, various aspects of God appear to him and he is able to understand these different aspects of God. Conscious realization of these aspects is what is meant by enumeration of God's names. Those who attain the realization of God in this way will undoubtedly go to Paradise, because Paradise is, in actual fact, the reward for the realization of God.

The term ninety nine in the tradition is purely symbolic. In reality, it means that there are countless names or attributes of God. Imām Rāzī in his commentary has quoted the opinions of certain religious scholars:

> *"God's names amount to five thousand." (Tafsīr Ibn Kathīr, vol. 1, p. 36).*

But the truth is that God has innumerable names.

In the tradition, the number of God's attributes (asmā' al-ḥusnā) is put at ninety nine. By studying the Quran, the scholars have discovered these, name by name. But these names do not denote the countless attributes of God. All these names, in fact, relate to human beings. The truth is that when the feeling of servitude awakens within man and God's consciousness becomes a reality then, naturally, different kinds of spiritual feelings arise within him. Naming the divine attributes, in fact, is an appropriate way of expressing these divine feelings.

For instance, a person reflects on his own existence, which is indeed an example of the best of moulds (95:4). He reflects on nature, in which everything is astonishingly a model of perfection. He reflects on the earth and the sky, and finds no defect in them (67:3). This thinking and observation create experiences for a person. He spontaneously feels that he should have the words which are appropriate to express these sublime feelings. At that time, the Quran, in exact accordance with his desire, gives him these words:

"Glory be to God, the Best of Creators." (23:14)

Formless God?

Divine attributes have in actual fact been enumerated to counter deviation, as has been mentioned in the Quran (7:180). Deviation has occurred mostly in philosophy. In philosophy God is conceived of as a Being without attributes. It is under the influence of this philosophical concept, that some have developed the concept of a formless God. The famous German philosopher, Friedrich Hegel (d. 1831) has expressed this as 'world spirit'. Another philosopher has called God an 'abstract idea'

According to this philosophic concept, God has no permanent and separate personality and is without attributes. That is to say, He is like 'gravity' or 'cosmic rays'. The Quran has mentioned God's names to refute this philosophic deviation, rather than purely to specify the divine names.

In philosophy, God has not been conceived of as a Creator, but rather that all the phenomena of creation are manifestations of God Himself. This is without doubt an abstract philosophic construct. It is obvious that in the universe diverse phenomena are to be found. This being so, it is baseless to conjecture that such a God, who is free from all kinds of attributes, may appear in the diverse forms of creation. Such contradictions prove that this concept of God is only a matter of philosophic conjecture. It has no scientific base in fact.

God and Scientific Study

In present times, consequent upon the scientific study of nature, the philosophic concept of God has been in effect rendered baseless. Today scientific study shows that in the universe there is perfect meaningfulness. This kind of meaningfulness could not be possible unless the Creator had a mind. Therefore, in science, without taking the name of God, it has been accepted that the one who has brought this universe into existence is an intelligent designer. (For details, see: Al-Risāla, 'Science and Theology', September 2007).

The truth is that the concept of God is interwoven in human nature, with diverse divine attributes. In scientific study, although the universe is, ultimately, different manifestations of the same unit, the atom, this atom astonishingly takes the form of different and opposite kinds of meaningful things. Both human nature and the external objects of the universe testify to the fact that there are great differences and diversities at the cosmic level and that at the same time in all these different elements of the universe there is an extraordinary harmony. In such a situation, the human mind desires to be able to conceive of God as having diverse attributes. The great names of God in the Quran answer this question.

The Great Attributes of God: The Answer to the Quest of Nature

A study of the great attributes of God shows that all these names of God are an introduction of God to man. Psychology has proved that man is by birth a seeking animal. By instinct he wants to find a superior being who will compensate for all of his shortcomings, and become the focus of his feelings and emotions.

The great attributes of God are indeed the answer to this question. These names of God are not a representation of the most superior God in any absolute sense. They rather introduce God in His relation to man. Therefore, when a person comes to know of these divine attributes with their full meaningfulness, he all of a sudden discovers that superior God that he had been seeking all along.

For instance, one of the divine names is al-Ghanī, that is, "Self-Sufficient," a Being who does not need anything from others, but rather has the power to fulfil the needs of everyone. This feeling is indwelling, consciously or unconsciously in every human being. Later, when a person learns that one of God's attributes is that He is self-sufficient, he immediately realizes that he has discovered the God he had been searching for all along. This is the reality which is expressed in this verse of the Quran:

"O men! It is you who stand in need of God—God is self-sufficient, and praiseworthy." (35:15)

Similarly, there is another feeling which is found in all human beings, consciously or unconsciously, and that is, everyone feels that he or she is a creature who is in need of sustenance. Sustenance means all those things on which human lives depend.

At all times an individual feels himself to be in need of many things—water, food, air, oxygen and light, etc. In this world, all these things are available in abundance and in the right proportions.

Man, by nature, wants to know who that Being is who provides for all the things he requires, without demanding anything from him. Man wants to fully acknowledge this superior Benefactor and with profound feelings of gratitude he wants to surrender himself before that Being. Here it is the great attributes of God which guide him.

One of the names of God is al-Razzāq, the Giver. When a person discovers God as the Giver, he feels, all of a sudden, that he has found the answer to his desire. This is the reality which has been expressed thus in the Quran: "It is God Who is the great Sustainer, the Mighty One, the Invincible." (51:58) Every person has yet another need. The present world in which an individual has to lead his life has been created in such a way that no one can live here in an ideal way. Under the influence of desires and wishes, individuals repeatedly make mistakes. In these situations a person thinks of how he might save himself from the feeling of guilt and how it might be possible to purify his soul. Here again, he finds the source of solace in the divine attributes.

As we know, one of God's names is al-Ghaffār, the Forgiver. It is in this concept of the Forgiver that one's mind finds solace. The following verse of the Quran guides us:

> *"God says, 'O My servants, who have committed excesses against their own souls, do not despair of God's mercy, for God surely forgives all sins. He is truly the Most Forgiving, the Most Merciful.'" (39:53)*

Connecting with God

All the divine names mentioned in the Quran give us points of reference for reflection and pondering. With these names we find definite guidance with which we may arrive at a concept of the divine Being, of the Being of God, and thinking of the attributes of God, we may establish a specific intellectual relationship with the Divine Being. It is this relationship which is called God-realization.

This is why the Quran tells us about the best names of God. It also tells us:

> *"God has the Most Excellent Names. Call on Him by His Names and keep away from those who distort them." (7:180).*

That is, think of God in terms of these perfect divine attributes, rather than by such names as people have themselves concocted.

What is God? God, in one respect, compensates for our helplessness. Man by his very nature lives in total helplessness, whereas God, because of being the Creator, the Lord, is All-powerful. As such, it is but natural that man should call upon Him on all occasions. For this purpose man is aided by his knowledge of God's great attributes.

All these names of God, in fact, relate to man. Whenever man is in need of divine succour, he makes reference to these names. Whenever any feelings awaken within man of his helplessness or of his servitude, or he has any kind of negative emotions, these divine names immediately give him some word which guides him. With these guiding words he gets connected with the Lord of the World just as by dialling a number on the telephone, one immediately gets connected with the desired person.

Calling out to God with His Names

It is a fact that a human being is a truth-seeking animal by nature. Very soon, there awakens within him a feeling that some superior being must exist who will grant him the light of guidance. At that time he calls out, "O God of guidance, grant me guidance by Your special mercy."

In this present world, man repeatedly faces such situations in which he feels himself helpless. At that time, under the influence of his latent feelings, he wants to call upon a superior being. Then of the best names he finds a divine name of the superior being such as relates to that particular situation in which he finds himself and with that in mind, he calls out: "O God, You alone are my helper, help me in all ways possible."

A human being cannot think in an abstract way. Because of his mental make-up a person always requires words by which he may bring concepts to mind. The same is true of God's names. These names do not denote the name of God in the absolute sense. They say only those names which we require as human beings. It is as if these divine names are to fulfil human needs, rather than to describe the higher reality that is the divine Being

Asmā' al-ḥusnā means attributes of God's names, but these divine names are not in the absolute sense an introduction to God; they introduce God in relation to man. Asmā' al-ḥusnā, in actual fact, give a person a point of reference for remembrance of God (dhikr) and prayer (du'ā'). For instance, if one needs food one may call upon God in these words—"O Razzāq, the Giver of food, provide me with food (rizq)." Similarly, when a person feels helpless, he may express himself by saying: "O Qādir, the All-powerful God! Compensate for my helplessness."

Not Mysterious

The general concept regarding asmā' al-ḥusnā is that they are some mysterious words. It is believed that some miraculous effect is hidden in these words, just as in the chants (mantras) of magicians, and that our task is only to remember them and recite them repeatedly. And then mysteriously we will receive miraculous benefits. This is what people think of divine names.

But this kind of concept of God's names is totally baseless. Asmā' al-ḥusnā are in no sense mysterious words. They represent a known and meaningful reality. Divine names are without doubt a great blessing for man. But there is nothing mysterious about it; rather it is a blessing which can be fully explained rationally.

Asmā' al-ḥusnā indeed are the known doors of God's mercy. These doors have been opened, as we learn from the Quran, that man may discover them and passing through them may reach the mercy of God in this world. Asmā' al-ḥusnā are like the good gates of the divine mercy. They are the means of connecting us to God. They are like a God-given key to ma'rifah, or God-realization, which awaken our hearts and minds and take us from darkness to light.

Asmā 'al-Ḥusnā (God's Best Names)

If a book were to be written giving the history of communication, it would include the role of the pigeon who took messages to people, the telegraph, the telephone and the mobile phone. On reading the book, whether or not the reader fully understands the language of the book, if he had not already seen that pigeon, telegraph, telephone or mobile phone, he would not be able to understand the reality of these things.

Any such book is informative for one who has some prior knowledge of these things, but for one who is poorly informed, this book will be little short of a mystery.

The same is true of God's beautiful names. God's good names have been mentioned in the Quran and the Hadith, but just a reading of these names in the Quran and the Hadith does not suffice. In spite of being mentioned in the Quran and the Hadith, all these names remain poorly understood. One can know the reality of these names only when one has acquired the knowledge of these things through one's own discovery. Without personal discovery, these names will be mere formalities, rather than a treasure house of the realization of God.

Calling upon God with His Greatest Name

Regarding asmā' al-ḥusnā a question asked by people is: "Has God one proper name (ism al-aʿẓam) or has God one main or great name? If that is so, what is it?" Different traditions have been recorded in the Hadith about ism al-aʿẓam. We give below two traditions by Imām Aḥmad:

1. Anas ibn Mālik narrated that, once the Prophet of Islam heard someone saying: "O God, I beseech You. All praise is for You. You are the object of worship, You have no partner. You have done great favours to man. You have created the earth and the heavens without any model. Greatness and Honour are Yours." On hearing this, the Prophet of Islam said: "You have called God with ism al-aʿẓam, when He is called in this way He will certainly answer your call, and when He is asked for anything in this way He grants it." (Musnad Aḥmad, Hadith No. 12205).

2. ʿAbd Allāh ibn Buraydah narrates that the Prophet Muḥammad heard someone say: "O God, I beseech You. I bear witness that You are God, there is no other person worthy of worship. You stand alone, You are self-sufficient. You have not given birth to anyone nor have You been born to someone. You have no equal." On hearing this, the Prophet observed: "He has made a

request to God with ism al-aʿẓam, if something is asked for with ism al-aʿẓam, He certainly grants it. And when the prayer is prefixed by it, He certainly accepts it." (Musnad Aḥmad, Hadith No. 22965).

In both the traditions along with the name of Allāh there are other names with divine attributes. This shows that ism al-aʿẓam cannot be just one name. Had it been one name, the prayer of the Prophet's Companion would also have mentioned only one name. But there are several names of God in this prayer (duʿāʾ). In spite of this clear indication, regarding ism al-aʿẓam to be only one main name of God, and making every effort to find that name, is without doubt a mistake.

The truth is that ism al-aʿẓam is not just one great name, but is rather a great state or feeling. In the above prayer the Companion did not repeat some words by rote, but rather in a great state of emotion, some particular words fell from his lips, and this is what is meant by calling upon God with ism al-aʿẓam. Ism al-aʿẓam relates in actual fact to spiritual or divine feelings. Calling upon God with such words as are full of feelings is calling upon God with ism al-aʿẓam.

Prayer in One's Mother Tongue

The previous hadith mentions the prayer of a Companion. The Prophet of Islam said that this prayer was a prayer with ism al-aʿẓam. Since this prayer was said by the Companion in the Arabic language, people consciously or unconsciously regard that a prayer with ism al-aʿẓam is one which is done in the Arabic language, and a prayer not said in the Arabic language is not the prayer of ism al-aʿẓam.

But this thinking is not right. In its reality, the prayers said by the Companions were in their own mother tongue, rather than in the Arabic language. Associating prayer with the Arabic language is an unnatural concept. Duʿāʾ, or prayer, is another name for the feelings of the heart, rather than just any linguistic sequence. The Quran tells us that "each Prophet was sent in the language of his own community." (14:4). The same is true of du'ā'. Just as the calling of people to God is done in the language of one's own community, du'ā' is also said in the mother tongue of the individual.

If prayer were associated with the Arabic language alone, and if the prayer in Arabic language were regarded as superior prayer, this would amount to nullifying the actual spirit of prayer. Prayer is not just the repetition of certain words. Prayer means calling upon God or praying to God with one's heart and mind, and such prayer will always come to one's lips only in one's mother tongue.

Prayer that Brings you Close to God

Du'ā' is not something technical. It is an external expression of an internal tempest. When a person discovers God in all His glory and greatness, then, while thinking of God, his feelings become so intense that he deeply realizes the presence of God; he feels as if he has reached the vicinity of God. When he undergoes this tumultuous experience, this in the hadith is described thus:

> *"Man remembered God in his solitude and, with the intensity of emotion, tears well up in his eyes." (Ṣaḥīḥ al-Bukhārī, Hadith No. 660)*

This hadith speaks of a person who thinks of this world as a testing ground, and deeply realizes the eventuality of death and the Day of Reckoning. Then he undergoes these spiritual feelings, when he keenly feels the fire of hell, and is able to see the eternal scenes of Paradise in his imagination. When he undergoes the deep experience of the remembrance of God, and becomes oblivious of everything else, all else besides God becomes totally unimportant in his eyes.

In such tumultuous moments he experiences a tempest in his heart and mind. In his eyes an ocean of tears well up in fear of God. When he stops thinking and only has a heightened sense of feeling, the divine nature latent within him finds words in the form of tears. In such tempestuous moments, whatever a person utters from his lips is genuine du'a', or prayer. It is this du'a' which is du'a' with ism al-a'zam and such a du'a' is always in one's own mother tongue, rather than in any other language.

Prayer from the Heart

Once I happened to meet a person, who told me that he had been seeking the answer to a question for the last ten years, but he had not yet succeeded in finding it. I asked him what his question was? He said, "I want to know what ism al-a'zam is?" Ism al-a'zam means a prayer that invokes God's greatest name. He told me that he had read many books, he had met many religious scholars and saints, but he had not yet received any satisfactory answer to the question. He said, "Now I have come to you. If possible, please give me the answer and ease my tension."

I said, "Your anxiety is purely self-induced. You have supposed that ism al-a'zam is like a mantra, that is, a magic formula. Now you want to know that mantra, but this will never happen."

I said that ism al-a'zam is not the name of some words but is rather the name of some state or feelings. The prayer said from the heart is prayer with ism al-a'zam. It is in actual fact the feeling of your own heart which makes a prayer a prayer of ism al-a'zam. No human word has the power to become God's ism al-a'zam, because it cannot encompass the unlimited being of God.

I said that there was once a person just like him. He was in search of some treasure. He found that this treasure was kept hidden in a palace on the peak of some mountain. And the gate of this palace was locked. This lock did not open with any key, but with a magic formula. Now he went in search of that mantra. He went on seeking and finally reached a place where he met a sadhu who knew this magic formula.

He requested the sadhu to tell him the mantra. The sadhu told him what it was. The sadhu said that the mantra was "sim sim". Then the sadhu told him to go to a particular mountain top where he would find the palace with its gate locked and then, in front of that gate, he had to say: "Khul ae sim sim, khul ae sim sim" (Open, O sim sim, Open, O sim sim) and then the lock would open. The seeker then set off. After a long journey, by the time he reached the palace gate, he had forgotten the mantra. He stood in front of the gate, and uttered somewhat similar sounding words like tam tam, dum dum, bum bum. But the gate did not open. Then he came back to the sadhu again. The sadhu told him that the mantra was wrong, that was why he could not unlock the gate. Now he had to go again and say, "sim sim". This time the man learnt it by rote and again traveled to that place. Now he stood in front of the palace gate and said "khul ae sim sim", and immediately the door opened.

Many people regard ism al-aʿẓam as a kind of magical word, but this is wrong. Indeed ism al-aʿẓam is not a name you will find in a dictionary; it is another name for the internal state of a person. Whenever any true servant of God prays to God with sublime feelings from the heart, he receives the support of angels. At that time, particular spiritual words come to his lips. That is what it is to pray with ism al-aʿẓam. This kind of duʿāʾ is guided by divine inspiration and the duʿāʾ which is said with divine inspiration will definitely come straight from the human heart.

The Prayer which God Accepts

The real duʿāʾ, or prayer, comes out of one's entire being, rather than from just the utterings of some words. It is a fact that the seeker or one who asks from God is never deprived. But asking does not mean just the repetition of certain words. The real asking is that in which man's entire being becomes a part of it. If someone says: "O God! Accept me," but does things which are not acceptable to God, then that is a proof that his request was not sincere.

If a child asked his mother for bread, it is not possible that his mother would place a burning coal in his hand. God is the most compassionate of all to His creatures. It is not possible that you ask God for a humble heart (khashyah) and that God would instead give you hardheartedness.

If you ask God for remembrance of Him, it is not possible that God would grant you forgetfulness of Him. If you want your sole concern to be the Hereafter, and then God grants you love of this world; if you want true religiosity from God it is not possible for God to give you a soulless religiosity. If you ask God for truthfulness, it is not possible that God would cause you to lead your life in the darkness of misguidance.

If in your life the thing that you desire the most is absent, this is a proof that you have not so far asked God for it. If you have to buy milk and you go to the market with a sieve then even after spending money you will come away empty handed. Similarly, if you keep repeating the words of prayer with your lips, but your real being gets diverted to something else then it would be right to say that neither had you asked nor had you received, for one who seeks finds.

It cannot be said of the Lord of the universe that He treats His people in such a way that when on Doomsday a person comes face to face with God, he looks at his Lord with intense regret (ḥasrah) and says: "O God, I asked You for something but you did not give it to me." By God, that is impossible, that is impossible, that is impossible! The Lord of the universe comes near you morning and evening with all His treasures and calls out: "Who is there? If you seek, I will give it to you." But those who want God's blessings and remain forgetful, then how can you blame the Giver?

Prayer that Can Change Destiny

According to a hadith: "Only duʿāʾ can change God's decision." (Sunan al-Tirmidhī, Hadith No. 2139) God has established the system of this world on the basis of cause and effect, and then God has given human beings total freedom. Now a person acts as he pleases and the good or evil results ensue either in agreement with or in opposition to the system of cause and effect set up by God. My belief is that this system is absolute. For no one can the system be set at naught.

In this matter, the only exception is that of du'ā', or sincere prayer. When a person prays to God and, given that God grants his prayer, then at that time God intervenes in the system of cause and effect and paves the way for a person according to his prayer to Him. This means that du'ā' changes God's decision (qaḍā' wa qadar).

But du'ā' is not just the repetition of certain words. Even if these prayers consist of verses from the Quran or from the traditions learnt by rote, it cannot be effective. To change the system of predetermination (qaḍā') such du'ā' is required as comes straight from the heart, in which the entire existence of an individual is involved, and his whole personality is shaken to the core.

Another condition for the acceptance of this kind of du'ā' is that the one who is praying has so purified himself intellectually that his thinking has risen to the same plane as divine thinking. Such a person will ask God for only that which is acceptable to Him. He will not say such prayers to God as are not in accordance with the way of God.

An Example of the Prophet's Prayer

All the prophets of God have said their prayers with ism al-a'ẓam. For instance, when on the occasion of the battle of Badr the Prophet of Islam looked at the battlefield, he saw that the enemy army was very strong as compared to the army of the believers. The believers lacked in weaponry, as well as were very small in number as compared to the enemy army. On seeing this inequality, the Prophet was emotionally very disturbed.

In total helplessness, he fell down in prostration before God. At that time, he uttered these words:

> "O God, if You destroy this group of believers, You will never be worshipped on the earth." (Musnad Aḥmad, Hadith No. 208).

This du'ā', in respect of the Prophet's godly feelings (rabbānī feelings), was a du'ā' with ism al-a'ẓam, which was accepted in the full sense. With the help of God the weaker group defeated the stronger group.

The prayer with ism al-aʿẓam is not peculiar only to the prophets. This prayer can be granted to every servant of God. Anyone who turns to God with sublime godly feelings in all sincerity, with full faith, may be granted the blessing of the prayer with ism al-aʿẓam. It can be recognized that on the occasion of such prayer, a person feels that his whole existence has bathed in the divine light. At that time he starts speaking such words as he may never previously have thought of. In history, there are many servants of God who have been granted the blessings of prayer with ism al-aʿẓam.

Prayer with Tears

Chapter 9 of the Quran mentions some believers who, on the occasion of the Tabūk campaign (8 AH), because it was a general call, wanted to serve in this campaign. But they had not enough money to prepare for this long journey. So they came to the Prophet for help, but the Prophet excused himself. This incident has been described in the Quran in this verse: "Nor [does any blame] attach to those who came to you to be provided with mounts, and when you said, 'I can find no mounts for you,' they went back, and tears welled up in their eyes with sadness, since they could not find any way to contribute." (9:92)

These Muslims could not take part in the Tabūk campaign, but according to one of the traditions of the Prophet, they were credited with having participated in this campaign. While coming back from this campaign, the Prophet said about them to his Companions:

> *"There are some people in Madinah who were with you,*
> *whatever path you traversed, whenever you spent some*
> *of your money, or whatever valley you crossed, they were*
> *with you." (Sunan Abī Dāwūd, Hadith No. 2508)*

This was a great reward which the believers of Madinah received, that is, being rewarded for participation in the action without their having participated in it. When I think about it, I feel that they received this unique reward because of their du'a' with ism al-a'zam.

I feel as if they must have prayed in these words with tears welling up in their eyes in solitude: "O God, the reward that You have given to others because of Your attribute of being just, give us that reward because of Your being merciful. The reward that You have given to others because of their deeds, give us that reward as a result of our prayers. What You have given to others because of deservation, give us that because of our asking for it. What You have given to others because of their ability, give us that because of our helplessness. What You have given to others because they are strong believers, grant us that because of our being weak in physical strength, because Your messenger has told us that 'even the weak believer has goodness in him.'"

Between God and Man

The beautiful names which God has chosen to introduce Himself to man are such as will open the gate of mercy to man. God's beautiful names tell us what the meeting points between God and man are. It is through these meeting points that man may achieve closeness with God. Then, if the spirit of God's servant is very great, this enables him in his prayer to God to make use of a great name of God and in so doing make divine closeness possible, just as by switching on an electric switch, the bulb immediately lights up.

There is nothing mysterious about this. The truth is that this is a law of nature, which we can understand by studying the relationship based on feelings and emotions between human beings themselves.

Prayer and Super Prayer

There are two kinds of calling upon God, or prayer. One is to utter some specific words in the simple sense and then ask God for something. The other is that which may be called super prayer. This is the kind in which the suppliant prays in such a manner that it becomes a personal issue for

God Himself, just as it was a personal matter for the caller. Where the first type of prayer is traditional, the second type of prayer is creative. The former type of prayer can be called making a request, whereas the latter may be called invoking God, for example: "Almighty God was invoked by His call."

This is the difference between simple prayer and prayer taking the great name of God. Prayer may be of a general kind but prayer taking the great name of God is a super prayer. For a better understanding of this matter, we give an example below.

An Example of Super Prayer

This example relates to a child who lived in Rampur, a city in U.P. (India). The child said to his father, "Please buy me a bicycle." The father's income was not sufficient for him to be able to afford to buy a bicycle, so he ignored the request. The child used to ask for a bicycle repeatedly, and the father repeatedly rejected his request. Finally, one day he scolded his son: "I have told you I cannot buy a bicycle. Don't talk to me about it again, otherwise I'll beat you." At this, the child's eyes filled with tears. He remained silent for some time. Then, in tears, he said: "You are my father. If I don't ask of you, then whom should I ask?" These words really touched his father. All of a sudden he was moved and said: "All right, son, I'll buy you a bicycle. I'll do it tomorrow." As he spoke his eyes also filled with tears. The next day he arranged for the loan of some money and got a bicycle for his son.

The son had apparently just uttered some words, but as he did so, his whole being had become one with his words. These words meant that he had totally surrendered himself to his guardian. These words brought him to the point where his son's request became as great an issue for the guardian as it was for the son. The words of the son brought the father face to face with the idea that if he did not give his son a bicycle, his fatherhood would be in question.

This incident leads us to understand what kind of prayer (du'ā') it is which attracts God's mercy to the caller. These are not words learned by rote. This prayer is one into which the caller has poured his whole being. When the caller weeps with helplessness, this cannot be borne either by the heavens or the earth. When a person becomes so close to his Lord that "the taker" and "the Giver" come on to the same plane, this is the moment when his prayer is not just a word out of the dictionary, but it is expressive of the caller's whole personality. At that time, God's blessings are showered upon the servant. Both the servant and the Lord become well content with one another. The All-Powerful embraces the all helpless.

The above incident illustrates both kinds of prayer. On the first occasion, when the child asked his father just to buy him a bicycle it was an ordinary prayer but, later, he cried and said, "You are my father. If I don't ask you, then whom should I ask?" When these words were spontaneously uttered by the child, it was like a super prayer. The words of the first kind of prayer did not influence his father, but the second kind of prayer just melted him. He was moved. He became so influenced that he was ready to buy the bicycle, even if he did not have enough money.

From this example we can understand the difference between a general kind of prayer and a prayer taking the great name of God. The general kind of prayer is just the uttering of some words, but prayer taking the great name of God is super prayer. Such prayer moves God Himself. According to a hadith the prayer of the oppressed one goes straight to heaven. The gates of heaven are opened for it. God Almighty says about the prayer of such a person, "By My honour, I will certainly fulfil his prayer, in due course." (Musnad Aḥmad, Hadith No. 8043)

The difference between prayer and super prayer is not that of wording. It is rather the difference in the inner spirit of the suppliant. In actual fact, it depends on the inner or internal condition of the caller, whether the prayer which he utters will become a super prayer or only a general prayer.

Exemplary Supplication

There are two kinds of prayers, examples of which are given below. One is the standard type of prayer which can be had in book form and learned by rote, then repeated at the appropriate times. For instance: "Our Lord, grant us good in this world as well as good in the world to come, and protect us from the torment of the fire." (The Quran, 2:201). This manner of prayer is an example of traditional supplication.

Then there is the example of a superior form of prayer. About 3,500 years ago an idolatrous king, the Pharaoh, ruled in Egypt. The Prophet Mūsā came to the world in those days and conveyed the message of monotheism to the Egyptians. The Pharaoh himself became a dire opponent of Mūsā, but his wife, Āsiyah bint Muzāḥim, believed in Mūsā and was influenced by his call to accept monotheism.

In ancient times, this was a matter of immense gravity. It was an age when people had to follow the religion of the king. In those times, following the state religion was a symbol of political loyalty. Anyone who did not believe in the state religion was considered a rebel and was punished as such. Today we live in an environment of religious freedom but in ancient times, for thousands of years, the system of religious persecution was prevalent throughout the world.

It was against this background that the Pharaoh gave the command to have his wife Āsiyah executed. The Quran tells us that at that time Āsiyah said this prayer to God:

> *"My Lord, build me a house in nearness to You in Paradise." (66:11)*

When we look at this prayer of Āsiyah in this context, it is like saying: "I sacrifice my seat in the palace of a worldly king. O Lord, give me a better seat in Your neighborhood in the world Hereafter." Scholars have commented: "How good is this prayer!" (Ṣafwah al-Tafāsīr, vol. 3, p. 412.

This prayer was without doubt a creative one. Āsiyah bint Muzāḥim had two alternatives: either the life of the palace adhering to the idolatrous religion of Pharaoh, or the monotheistic religion of God—which would lead to her being brutally killed. At that time Āsiyah's realization of God had ascended to such a level that she took no time in deciding that, for the sake of truth, she must abandon the temporary palace of this world and opt for the eternal Paradise of God, even if she were to be executed as the price for her choice.

Looked at against this background, Āsiyah bint Muzāhim's prayer was without doubt a superior prayer. It was immediately accepted. According to a tradition, before her death the angels showed her the palace she was to be given by God in Paradise. Therefore, Āsiyah gave up her life with her face reflecting happiness, contentment and peace.

Āsiyah bint Muzāhim's prayer is recorded in the Quran. It is not just the prayer of an individual but is rather an exemplary supplication of universal application. The truth is that every man and woman should pray like this. All men and women have to pass through this stage. All men and women must each say at the level of sacrifice, "O God, I sacrifice my worldly things for the sake of Your religion, so that in the next stage of life You give me a better reward." These are the men and women about whom it will be proclaimed on the Day of Judgement that they forsook the temporary Paradise for the sake of God and now enter into the superior Paradise of the Hereafter, so that they may live in happiness and comfort eternally and never have to suffer from any kind of mental or physical discomfort.

True Prayer: A Living Experience

It is only by the grace of God that one may pray, taking the great name of God. Such grace is bestowed only upon one who experiences the greatness of God before setting himself to pray. Taking the great name of God in prayer has no mystery about it. It only means that the suppliant, being a seeker after truth, has found the truth in the form of God and then his state is described in the Quran as "one who was dead, to whom We gave life, and a light whereby he could walk among people." (6:122)

Verse 33 of chapter 41 of the Quran asks a rhetorical question about such a human being as lives in the remembrance of God:

"Who speaks better than one who calls to God and says, 'I am surely of those who submit.'"

That is, he is one who remembers God all the time, thinks of God all the time and experiences glimpses of God at every moment. On extraordinary occasions, he gives vent to his latent spiritual feelings in a torrent of words. At that time, he starts calling on God in inspired words of a special kind. This is taking the great name of God in prayer. It is the inspiration of a righteously prepared mind.

An Incident Relating to a Virtuous Lady

As mentioned above, Pharaoh's wife Āsiyah bint Muzāḥim secretly believed in the religion of the Prophet Mūsā. When Pharaoh learnt of this, he became incensed and commanded her execution. At that time Āsiyah said this prayer which has been set forth in the Quran:

"My Lord, build me a house in nearness to You in Paradise and save me from Pharaoh and his misdeeds. Save me from all evil-doers." (66:11)

This is a prayer which is fully imbued with the spirit of ism al-aʿẓam, the greatest name of God. In some traditions, it has been recorded that when Āsiyah said this prayer, before her death she was shown her home by the angels in Paradise which she was to be awarded in the Hereafter. (al-Qurṭubī, vol. 18, p. 203)

It is certain that this prayer of Āsiyah did not come out of her lips all of a sudden but rather reflected the experiences she had undergone in her life. Prior to this prayer, she had become a prepared or realized personality. She lived even before this prayer in the remembrance of God. This was why when she came to know of the utmost cruelty of Pharaoh, these rabbānī (divine) words came out quite naturally from her lips.

A Historical Example

Sulṭān ʿAbd al-Raḥmān al-Nāṣir (d. 961) once ruled Andalusia (Spain). He built a very grand palace at Cordova, which took twenty five years to complete. This palace was four miles long and three miles wide. It was named "al-Zahrā'." But because of its being extraordinarily large, it came to be called Madīnat al-Zahrā' (the city of al-Zahrā'), instead of the palace of al-Zahrā'.

Sulṭān ʿAbd al-Raḥmān al-Nāṣir was greatly interested in building monuments. He established this royal colony in the name of al-Zahrā' and built grand palaces in it. During their construction, the Sultan was so preoccupied that for three Fridays in succession he was not able to reach the mosque for the Friday prayer. On the fourth Friday, when the Sultan reached the Jāmiʿ Masjid, Qāḍī Mundhir (d. 966) preached the sermon in his presence and, without naming him, he strongly criticized the King.

Qāḍī Mundhir recited those verses of the Quran in which there were warnings about worldly constructions and about being oblivious of the Hereafter. For example,

> *"Do you build monuments on every high place in vanity, and erect castles hoping that you will live forever? When you lay hands upon anyone, you do so as tyrants. So fear God, and obey me." (26:128-131)*

> *"Who is better, he who founds his building on the fear of God and His good pleasure, or he who builds on the brink of a crumbling precipice, so that his house is ready to fall with him into the Fire of Hell? God does not guide the wrongdoers: the buildings which they have built will never cease to be a source of deep disquiet in their hearts, until their hearts are cut to pieces. God is All-Knowing and Wise." (9:109-110)*

Moreover, Qāḍī Mundhir recited a number of traditions to the same effect and explained them. In his sermon, although he did not name the

King, everyone who was saying his prayers in the mosque knew who was targeted by such strong criticism.

Everyone finds it difficult to take criticism but when criticism is voiced in a public gathering, it becomes intolerable. Furthermore, this criticism was done by an underling and the target was the ruler. When a ruler listens to criticism by his servant, his ego is affected. The religious people as well as others may fail to control themselves, but the Sultan controlled himself although he had greatly disliked this criticism. But he did not utter a word in the mosque and left the mosque quietly.

When he reached home, the Sultan said to his elder son, al-Ḥakam, "Today Qāḍī Mundhir has hurt me greatly. Now I have decided never to say my prayers behind him." Al-Ḥakam said: "Whether Qāḍī Mundhir is the Imām or not, since you have appointed him, it is in your power to depose him and replace him with another Imām, who does not dare to make such insolent remarks." On hearing this, the Sultan became angry. He scolded his son and said: "Woe to you, is it possible for one who is in error (referring to himself) to depose a virtuous man like Qāḍī Mundhir who has so many qualities, just for his own happiness? This can never happen."

"Since I was hurt by his harsh words, I have decided not to say my prayers behind him. Now it is my desire that I should atone for this oath that I have taken never to say my prayers behind him. Indeed, Qāḍī Mundhir in our lifetime, and in his lifetime will keep leading the prayer." Therefore, Qāḍī Mundhir continued to lead the Friday prayer even after the death of ʿAbd al-Raḥmān al-Nāṣir; his son did not depose him either. (Tārīkh Quḍāt al-Andalus, p. 70)

The above-mentioned incident has a great lesson in it. It shows what qualities are desirable for a person if he has to pray to God so that He accepts his prayer.

If the prayer is accepted by God its role is only fifty per cent, while the spiritual capability of the person who prays has a fifty per cent role in it. This spiritual capability existed in both Qāḍī Mundhir as well as in Sulṭān 'Abd al-Raḥmān. That is why one great du'ā' by Sulṭān 'Abd al-Raḥmān was accepted by God.

Prayer at Difficult Moments

During the rule of Sulṭān 'Abd al-Raḥman al-Nāṣir of Andalusia, Spain was afflicted by a drought. Mere survival became very difficult. The Sultan sent an important person to Qāḍī Mundhir to request him to lead the Ṣalāt al-Istisqā' (the prayer to God to give His blessing of rain). The Ṣalāt al-Istisqā' is a prayer, consisting of two units, performed during the time of drought to ask God for rain. Qāḍī Mundhir asked the messenger of the King: "What was the Sultan himself doing when he sent me the message about prayer?"

The messenger said, "I have never seen him more God-fearing than on this occasion. He is very disturbed. He is in solitude. I have seen him lying prostrate on the ground. His eyes were wet with tears. He acknowledged his sins and he was saying to God in prayer: 'O God, my forehead is in Your hand.' (he had prostrated himself with his forehead on the ground) 'Will You punish the people for my sins?'"

On hearing this, Qāḍī Mundhir felt relieved. He said to the messenger: "Go with rain, certainly it will rain today, because when the ruler of the earth bows in supplication, the Ruler of the Heaven will certainly show mercy." And so it happened. By the time the messenger reached home, rain had started falling. (al-Kāmil fī al-Tārīkh, vol. 7, p. 347)

Drought takes place on the earth, so that the dryness of eyes may be replaced with tears. The clouds thunder in the skies, so that people's hearts may tremble with the fear of the Lord. Heat becomes intense so that people may be reminded of the fire of Hell.

Such events have a deep relation with the asmā' al-ḥusnā and ism al-a'ẓam. If such events develop spiritual feelings within a person, he is granted the blessings of being able to call God the Lord of the world with the greatest prayer.

Invoking God's Infinite Mercy

By the grace of God, I have frequently had significant experiences. On December 30, 2006, I went to Lodhi Gardens with certain CPS members. It was in the nature of a spiritual outing for us. On this occasion, a duʿāʾ came out of my lips, which as I understood it was a duʿāʾ of ism al-aʿẓam.

When we reached the Lodhi Gardens I asked one of my team members, "When you entered the garden what was your first impression, or feeling?" People mentioned different experiences, then I said that when I entered this beautiful garden, I felt as if I was looking at Paradise from a distance. This beautiful garden for me became a distant introduction to Paradise.

Then I said with tears in my eyes: "O God, when You have brought me to this imperfect paradise, then by Your grace, help me to enter the perfect Paradise also." I added, "O God, my companions and I are the least deserving candidates for Paradise. If You, in spite of our total lack of merit, give us entry into Paradise, then this event would be akin to a new expression of Your attribute of mercy. The whole earth and the heavens and all the angels will be surprised to know that the ocean of God's mercy was so vast that even such undeserving people as us could not remain deprived of God's boundless mercy. How boundless was Your mercy that it enveloped even the most undeserving!"

You Have Been Granted Your Request, Mūsā

It was probably 1962. I had the opportunity to attend an important function in Anjaan Shaheed, a town in Azamgarh. Many Muslim scholars were present on this occasion. I had not been informed in advance that I had to address the gathering. Then quite without warning a group of people took me on to the stage and asked me to speak. There was no avoiding this. It was perhaps the first occasion when in the matter of making speeches that I experienced total helplessness. Earlier I had addressed gatherings repeatedly, but all these addresses had been in the form of reading out papers. Had I known in advance about this programme, I would have written an article to be read out on that occasion.

But this time I faced a situation in which I had to speak compulsorily without any prior preparation and I had to speak extempore. At that time, all of a sudden I started getting ideas about what to say.

I just remembered God and, in a frenzied manner, I started speaking. I began my speech with these words: There are many stories of prophets recorded in the Quran but these are not just historical stories. They have a lesson for our present life. One of these incidents, or stories is that God commanded Mūsā to go to the court of the tyrant king of Egypt and call upon him to accept monotheism.

The Prophet Mūsā said to God, "My breast is constricted and my tongue is not fluent." (The Quran, 26:13) Then by the grace of God Almighty, he prayed, "My Lord, open up my heart and make my task easy for me, loosen the knot in my tongue, so that they may understand what I have to say." (The Quran, 20:25–28)

I said that when Mūsā called upon the All-Hearing (al-Samīʿ) and the All-Seeing (al-Baṣīr), his call went straight to the divine throne and then God said, "You have been granted your request, Mūsā." (20:36)

Then, still in a frenzied state, I said that this event was not just a story from the past. This event was a living reality even today, just as God is ever present. Today also if a servant of God calls and says, "O God my breast is constricted and my tongue is not fluent," then again, his call will reach God, the All-Hearing, the All-Seeing, and he will be answered thus: "O My servant, the request you have made has been granted." As I said this, my eyes filled with tears. Then I went on speaking and kept on speaking at length, albeit extempore.

This event was like a breakthrough for me. Subsequently, I stopped writing everything down and started speaking extempore. Later, I participated in many national and international gatherings, conferences and delivered long speeches. It was undoubtedly the miracle of the du'a' on the occasion of the gathering of Anjaan Shaheed.

As I understand it, this du'a' was one with ism al-a'ẓam. Earlier I had been unable to speak extempore. But after this experience, I was able to address audiences. This can be explained only by believing that my prayer had been heard by God.

Be a Playback Speaker For Me

When I was travelling in some western country, I was invited to address a gathering, but I had not been told about what kind of audience it would be. I was just told that the audience would be composed of educated people. Due to some misunderstanding, I thought that the audience would be composed of people from India and Pakistan and, therefore, I could speak in Urdu.

When I reached there in the evening, I saw that many people were sitting in a big hall. On inquiring about them, I was told that they were all English-speaking people, and that I would have to address them in English because they did not understand Urdu. For me this news was like a bolt from the blue. Earlier, I had read only prepared papers in English. I had never spoken extempore in English in any gathering.

Very perturbed, I went to a side room and locked the door. Then I performed my ablutions and said two units of prayer Ṣalāt al-Ḥājah. This is a prayer which is said to ask God for something. When I raised my hand to my eyes they were so full of tears that it was as if a tap had been turned on.

Weeping, I said to God that I was totally helpless and I had to represent an Omnipotent God: "O God, if You command, even the stones will speak out and convey Your message. If You command, even the trees will break their silence and will address mankind. If You command, the earth and the heavens will say what man should have spoken. But, O God, because of the law of test You will never do this. Therefore, now You have no other choice but to help a helpless man like me. Your help should be so great as You have never given anyone before.

O God, in the name of all Your good names, I pray to You to become a playback speaker for me. You speak and I will repeat. Speak in a silent language, and I will repeat Your words. O God, if I do not speak on this occasion, it will be like fleeing from the battlefield, and if You do not help me today, this announcement (of calling people to God) will not be made in a way that is most desirable for You. O God, it is a moment when neither do I have a choice nor do You. O God, this is the moment when the total helplessness of man and the Omnipotence of God, the Creator, have arrived at one level. In such a situation, neither can I renege nor do You have the choice to ignore me."

After saying these prayers, I came out and sat on the speaker's chair in the hall. The whole hall was full of people and I was the only speaker. I started speaking in a frenzied manner, and, for about an hour, I continued to speak in English. The whole speech was extempore and fluent. At the end of the speech, I asked the audience if anyone wanted to ask a question. But no question came from the audience. Later someone told me that the audience had been so mesmerized by my language that they just did not dare to ask a question.

After this experience, my life quite unexpectedly entered upon a new phase, that is, I started speaking in English extempore. Speaking in English, giving interviews in English, making speeches in English, all these things had earlier not been a part of my life. Now they became part and parcel of my life and, by the grace of God, this situation still continues.

It was in 1947, when India gained its freedom that I started learning English. But I got no encouragement from anyone. My cousins laughed at me. At that time I was about 30 years of age, so everyone laughed at how I could think of learning a new language at that age. As a matter of common experience, they were right. But by divine succour everything is possible, for I believe, the prayer I made above was without doubt, a prayer with ism al-aʿẓam and it is due to the miracle of this prayer that something unexpected became a reality.

Islamic Literature in the Modern Idiom

Professor Muḥammad Mujīb (1985) was one of the three pillars of Jamia Millia Islamia in New Delhi. The others were Dr. Zakir Ḥusain (1969) and Dr. ʿĀbid Ḥusain (1978). Professor Mujīb was highly educated. He had an extraordinary command of the English language and had read the literature of the orientalists in detail.

It was in 1970 that I met Professor Mujīb on the campus of Jamia Millia. Professor Anwar ʿAlī Khān Soz (1987) was with me at that time. In the course of the conversation Professor Mujīb said in his inimitable style: "Maulvi Sahab, do you know that in this day and age Islam is being represented by Jewish scholars?"

What he wanted to point out was that in modern times a new style or idiom had been created. But that Muslim scholars had failed to produce Islamic literature in this new style and this task had been performed by educated Jews. They wrote books on various aspects of Islam in the modern idiom, although in many of these books Islamic teachings have been presented in a distorted form. But because in style they are in the modern idiom, educated people who wanted to study Islam in the English language often studied these books written by Jewish scholars.

I listened intently to Professor Mujīb. I did not answer him but on hearing what he had to say a tempest was stirred up in my mind. I came home silently and began to pray day and night saying, "O God grant me the ability to present to the world Your religion in the modern idiom. Help me to prepare literature on Islam in the modern idiom."

I often pray with specific reference to some incident. In this matter, too, I did likewise. After India's independence the Zamindari abolition act was implemented in Uttar Pradesh. Under the national government the new law was based on the principle, that whoever tilled the land, owned the land.

My family hailed from Azamgarh in UP. My family was one of the big landlords of the area. Most of our lands had been given to farmers to cultivate and then they paid some agricultural rent (lagaan). Now, according to the law of the Zamindari abolition act, the landlord (Zamindar) could get his land back only if the farmer who was tilling that land put it in writing that he was willing to relinquish the land.

Most of our land was with the farmers. All these farmers were Hindus. The manager of our land was also a Hindu named Bhau Ram. Bhau Ram was the most loyal employee of our family. He launched a campaign to get all the farmers who were tilling our land to give up their claim to the land in writing. Bhau Ram worked day and night to get these affidavits. It was exceptional that all our land was thus saved.

In those times Bhau Ram was in a frenzied state. He used to say to us: Babu jimdaari mein dagh na lage. (Zamindari should not become tainted, that is losing a piece of land was unacceptable). With reference to this incident, I began praying to God. I used to cry and say, "O God, Your religion too is getting tainted. Your religion is not being presented in the modern idiom which can address modern minds. Please grant me the ability to remove any stain from Your religion by presenting Islam in the modern style. With a perturbed mind and eyes full of tears, I used to pray day in and day out and I used to work hard to prepare myself."

In those times I was so restless that once I went to the Delhi Public Library, where I started reading books in the reference section of the library. At that time my absorption was so great that I did not even take a seat. I would just stand by the side of the bookshelves and read books one after another. At that time the weather was very cold and I caught a chill and fell ill. Then I had to take rest for about two months.

Today, I pen these lines, I can say that by the grace of God, I have written books on almost every Islamic subject, which, in a contemporary style effectively introduce Islam to the educated. Scholars both in the East and in the West have acknowledged this.

Now people are feeling the importance of such literature to the extent that they have devoted their lives to spreading this literature throughout different parts of the world. There are some American educated Muslims who have voluntarily placed all my books and the Al-Risala monthly magazine on the internet. Now in any part of the world anyone can read my writings both in Urdu and English.

There are also some Egyptian Arabs who are putting my books on the internet. Now, by the grace of God, my Arabic books can also be accessed on the internet everywhere. Moreover, in India, a whole team has devoted itself to this mission. In this way, this work is spreading fast at a global level. Certain educated people have attached such great importance to this literature that on their own initiative they have included my programme in Urdu and English and my speeches on television.

The coming into existence of this Islamic literature in a contemporary style was indeed an extraordinary event for such a powerless person with no resources. The only way that this happening can be explained is that a prayer (du'ā') with ism al-a'zam came to my heart with great fervour and God accepted it. It was in this way that it became possible for me to introduce Islam in modern times—an event which, at the outset, had seemed unthinkable for an individual like myself.

Asking from God in Utter Helplessness

It was October 24, 2006. It was the day of 'Īd. I had gone to a New Delhi mosque to perform my 'Īd prayer. There I was sitting in a corner in the mosque. And with tears in my eyes, I was praying with great feeling and emotion. I was reminded of a tradition, which is mentioned thus in a hadith:

"When the 'Īd day comes, God takes pride before the angels, and He says: 'O My angels, what is the reward for these people who have performed this act?' Then the angels say: 'O My Lord, the reward is that they should be fully recompensed for their actions.' God says, 'O My angels, My servants, men and women have discharged their duties and they have come calling upon me with du'ā'. By My Honour and by My Majesty, by My Glory, by My High Position, I will certainly listen to their call.' Then God says, 'Go back home, I have given you salvation and I have converted your bad deeds into good deeds.' In this way, they came back with their sins forgiven." (Shu'ab al-Īmān, al-Bayhaqī, Hadith No. 3444)

I was reminded of this hadith and while thinking about this hadith I was moved that God was giving great rewards to people today, but these rewards were for those who had done some good deed and I had no such good deed to my credit.

Then I was reminded of another incident regarding Sir Sayyad Aḥmad Khān (1898), founder of the Aligarh Muslim University. He once visited a Muslim Nawab for a donation for his then planned Muhammadan College (now Aligarh Muslim University). The Nawab Sahab was against some of Sir Sayyad's ideas and he refused to meet him. But Sir Sayyad was not deterred. He knew that in the evening the Nawab Sahab had an outing in his horse-drawn carriage. At that time, the beggars would line the road in front of the bungalow. Nawab Sahab used to give something or the other to everyone.

Sir Sayyad reached there in the evening and, sitting with the beggars, he turned his cap upside down like the bowl which beggars keep before them. The Nawab Sahab came out as usual in his horse-drawn carriage. Then he saw Sir Sayyad sitting in the line of beggars. At this the Nawab Sahab was quite shocked. He said, "Sayyad, how is it that you are here?" Sir Sayyad replied: "Nawab Sahab, if you cannot give me a donation, you can give me alms." The Nawab Sahab was moved at this. He got down from his carriage and took Sir Sayyad to his home. He gave him a large donation for the College.

Referring to this event I said, "O God, if I don't deserve anything on the basis of my actions, then grant me Your reward as alms for, in the Quran, You have said that just as the one who performs a good deed deserves a reward, similarly one who asks for something is also held deserving of reward. If You give not only to the person who has done something, but also to the person who is just making a request, then certainly I can hope that You will treat me accordingly."

I think that this is also an example of a duʿāʾ with ism al-aʿẓam, which God granted that I should do by His grace and mercy. So far as my experience goes, duʿāʾ with ism al-aʿẓam is not at all a repetition of words, learned by rote and neither is it a duʿāʾ which one can think of in advance. This kind of duʿāʾ is a direct blessing from God and it is like an inspiration which comes to one's mind all of a sudden.

Asmāʾ al-Ḥusnā - The 99 Names of God

1. al-Raḥmān (The All-Compassionate)
2. al-Raḥīm (The All-Merciful)
3. al-Malik (The Absolute Ruler)
4. al-Quddūs (The Pure One)
5. al-Salām (The Source of Peace)
6. al-Mu'min (The Inspirer of Faith)
7. al-Muhaymin (The Guardian)
8. al-ʿAzīz (The Victorious)
9. al-Jabbār (The Compeller)
10. al-Mutakabbir (The Supreme / The Greatest)
11. al-Khāliq (The Creator)
12. al-Bāri' (The Maker of Order)
13. al-Muṣawwir (The Shaper of Beauty)
14. al-Ghaffār (The Forgiving)
15. al-Qahhār (The Subduer)
16. al-Wahhāb (The Giver of All)
17. al-Razzāq (The Sustainer)
18. al-Fattāḥ (The Opener)
19. al-ʿAlīm (The Knower of All)
20. al-Qābiḍ (The Constrictor)
21. al-Bāsiṭ (The Reliever)
22. al-Khāfiḍ (The Abaser)
23. al-Rāfiʿ (The Exalter)
24. al-Muʿizz (The Bestower of Honors)
25. al-Mudhill (The Humiliator)
26. al-Samīʿ (The Hearer of All)

27. al-Baṣīr (The Seer of All)

28. al-Ḥakam (The Judge)

29. al-ʿAdl (The Just)

30. al-Laṭīf (The Subtle One)

31. al-Khabīr (The All-Aware)

32. al-Ḥalīm (The Forbearing)

33. al-ʿAẓīm (The Magnificent)

34. al-Ghafūr (The Forgiver and Hider of Faults)

35. al-Shakūr (The Rewarder of Thankfulness)

36. al-ʿAlī (The Highest)

37. al-Kabīr (The Greatest)

38. al-Ḥāfiẓ (The Preserver)

39. al-Muqīt (The Nourisher)

40. al-Ḥasīb (The Accounter)

41. al-Jalīl (The Mighty)

42. al-Karīm (The Generous)

43. al-Raqīb (The Watchful One)

44. al-Mujīb (The Responder to Prayer)

45. al-Wāsiʿ (The All-Comprehending)

46. al-Ḥakīm (The Perfectly Wise)

47. al-Wadūd (The Loving One)

48. al-Majīd (The Majestic One)

49. al-Bāʿith (The Resurrector)

50. al-Shahīd (The Witness)

51. al-Ḥaqq (The Truth)

52. al-Wakīl (The Trustee)

53. al-Qawī (The Possessor of All Strength)

54. al-Matīn (The Forceful One)

55. al-Walī (The Governor / Protecting Friend)

56. al-Ḥamīd (The Praised One)

57. al-Muḥṣī (The Appraiser)

58. al-Mubdi' (The Originator)

59. al-Muʿīd (The Restorer)

60. al-Muḥyī (The Giver of Life)

61. al-Mumīt (The Taker of Life)

62. al-Ḥayy (The Ever Living One)

63. al-Qayyūm (The Self-Existing One)

64. al-Wājid (The Finder)

65. al-Mājid (The Glorious)

66. al-Wāḥid (The Unique, The Single)

67. al-Aḥad (The One, The Indivisible)

68. al-Ṣamad (The Satisfier of All Needs)

69. al-Qādir (The All Powerful)

70. al-Muqtadir (The Creator of All Power)

71. al-Muqaddim (The Expediter)

72. al-Mu'akhkhir (The Delayer)

73. al-Awwal (The First)

74. al-Ākhir (The Last)

75. al-Ẓāhir (The Manifest One)

76. al-Bāṭin (The Hidden One)

77. al-Walī (The Protecting Friend)

78. al-Mutaʿālī (The Supreme One)

79. al-Barr (The Doer of Good)

80. al-Tawwāb (The Guide to Repentance)

81. al-Muntaqim (The Avenger)

82. al-ʿAfūw (The Forgiver)

83. al-Raʾūf (The Clement)

84. Mālik al-Mulk (The Owner of All)

85. Dhū al-Jalāl wa al-Ikrām (The Lord of Majesty and Bounty

86. al-Muqsiṭ (The Equitable One)

87. al-Jāmiʿ (The Gatherer)

88. al-Ghanī (The Rich One)

89. al-Mughnī (The Enricher)

90. al-Māniʿ (The Preventer of Harm)

91. al-Ḍārr (The Creator of the Harmful)

92. al-Nāfiʿ (The Creator of Good)

93. al-Nūr (The Light)

94. al-Hādī (The Guide)

95. al-Badīʿ (The Originator)

96. al-Bāqī (The Everlasting One)

97. al-Wārith (The Inheritor of All)

98. al-Rashīd (The Righteous Teacher)

99. al-Ṣabūr (The Patient One)